The

LEGACY OF
JOHN CALVIN

The Calvin 500 Series

LEGACY OF
JOHN CALVIN

HIS INFLUENCE ON
THE MODERN WORLD

DAVID W. HALL

PUBLISHING
P.O. BOX 817 • PHILLIPSBURG • NEW JERSEY 08865-0817

Library of Congress Cataloging-in-Publication Data
Hall, David W., 1955-
The legacy of John Calvin : his influence on the modern world / David W. Hall.
        p. cm. — (The Calvin 500 series)
Includes bibliographical references.
ISBN-13: 978-1-59638-085-1 (pbk.)
1. Calvin, Jean, 1509–1564—Influence. 2. Civilization, Modern. I. Title.
BX9418.H275 2008
284'.2092—dc22
                                2008005001

To all our friends around the world who helped make Calvin 500 possible; especially to Ambassador Faith Whittlesey, Guillaume Taylor, and the Parish Council of St. Pierre Cathedral, our gracious hosts in Geneva.

CONTENTS

A Chronology of John Calvin's Life

1509	Born in Noyon (July 10)
1521	Enrolled in the *College de Montaigu* in Paris
1528–33	Studied law in Bourges and Orleans
1532	Published *De Clementia* (first book, a commentary on Seneca)
1533–34	Experienced a sudden conversion; fled Paris
1534	Resigned his Roman Catholic chaplaincy
1534–35	Resided in Basle
1536	Composed first edition of *Institutes of the Christian Religion* (March)
1536	Arrived (July) and settled in Geneva as pastor
1538–41	Exiled to Strasbourg (April); pastored Protestant exiles there
1540	Married Idelette de Bure
1541	Returned to Geneva (September 13); drafted his *Ecclesiastical Ordinances*
1542	Appointed to a committee to revise the Genevan Edicts

	Birth of Calvin's son (July 28), Jacques, who lived only two weeks
	Published "The Form of Church Prayers," an early Reformed liturgy
1543	Received a home near St. Pierre from Genevan civic leaders
	Published *The Bondage and Liberation of the Will; On the Necessity for Reforming the Church*
1544	Published a *Brief Instruction . . . Against the Anabaptists*
1549	Death of Idelette Calvin; Theodore Beza relocated to Geneva
1550	Published *Concerning Scandals*
1558	Founded the Academy of Geneva (dedication service in June 1559)
1559	Revised and completed final edition of *Institutes of the Christian Religion*
1564	Death of Calvin (May 27)

Ten Ways Modern Culture Is Different because of John Calvin

An international celebration of the five hundredth anniversary of John Calvin's birth (and the 450th anniversary of the final edition of his magisterial *Institutes of the Christian Religion*) will commence in 2009 (see www.calvin500.org online for more information). For those who have heard little or primarily negative things about the Genevan Reformer, an obvious question might be "why?" A brief review of ten areas of culture that were irrevocably changed by the influence of Calvin and his band of brothers is in order. Love him or hate him, Calvin was a change agent—and one whose influence was for the better. The light Calvin brought to society made the world a fundamentally different place after his life's work began to be displayed.

Some, in a day that was less prejudiced, thought that Calvin's accomplishments were dramatic. Writing in the middle of the nineteenth century, Harvard Professor George Bancroft ranked Calvin among "the foremost of modern republican legislators," who was responsible for elevating the culture of Geneva into "the impregnable fortress of popular liberty, the fertile seed-plot of democracy." Bancroft even credited the "free institutions of America" as being derived "chiefly from Calvinism through the medium of Puritanism." Moreover, he traced the living legacy of Calvin among the Plymouth pilgrims, the Huguenot settlers of South Carolina, and the Dutch colonists in Manhattan, concluding: "He that will not honor the memory and respect the influence of Calvin knows but little of the origin of American liberty."[1]

Calvinism, when all is over and done with, may be more worthy of international celebrations than many other movements. When various ideological movements throughout history are assessed, the Genevan Reformer's positive cumulative impact is greater than that of Rousseau, Nietzsche, Marx, and many other philosophers. Certainly, few if any ministers or theologians will make greater contributions to political, societal, or cultural change than did Calvin.

Careful thinkers and students of history may even find the quincentenary of Calvin's birth to be an opportune time to evaluate the correctness of C. S. Lewis's surprising comment that modern observers need to comprehend "the freshness, the audacity, and (soon) the fashionableness of Calvinism."[2] That is a well-placed challenge. Moreover, that fashionableness to which Lewis refers may explain how and why even some of the most stridently anti-Calvinist thinkers of a later day—venomous enemies of Calvinism, actually, like Thomas Jefferson—would employ mottoes from the Calvinistic Huguenots of old to justify resistance to tyrants on American shores. Even if contemporary researchers remain studiously blind to Calvin's immense legacy, there may have been a day when his legacy

---

1. George Bancroft, "A Word on Calvin, the Reformer," in his *Literary and Historical Miscellanies* (New York, 1855), 405ff; cited in Philip Schaff, *History of the Christian Church*, 8 vols. (1910; repr. Grand Rapids: Eerdmans, 1979), 8:522.

2. Cited by Alister McGrath, *A Life of John Calvin* (Cambridge, MA: Basil Blackwell Ltd., 1990), 247.

was far more apparent. We can be forgiven if our concerted aim is to rehabilitate an image that actually gave us much good.

There are two kinds of leaders: (1) those who predict future changes, and (2) those who change future predictions. The first type sees trends and quickly claims a place on the leading edge of change, thereby fitting in with those inevitable trends. That is the kind of leader who senses the direction of a parade and runs to be at the head of the procession. The second type—and Calvin was certainly one of these—observes the trajectory but determines that it needs correction. Calvin was an event-maker who changed the parade route and left a very large imprint on Western history. Below are ten short summaries of some of the changes produced as a result of his legacy. As you will see, life after Calvin was irrevocably different than it had been before him.

If, indeed, the reader has a higher appreciation for Calvin after beginning with his accomplishments in this section, he or she would do well to continue on to the brief sketch of Calvin's life in part 2 followed by tributes from some unexpected quarters in part 3 below.

1. Education: The Academy

Calvin broke with medieval pedagogy that limited education primarily to an aristocratic elite. His Academy, founded in 1559, was a pilot program in broad-based education for the city. Although Genevans had sought for two centuries to establish a university, only after Calvin's settlement there did a college finally succeed.[3]

---

3. The most recent history of this university recounts several abortive efforts, including one in 1420 under Roman Catholic authority and the attempt by Francois de Versonnex in 1429. See Marco Marcacci, *Histoire de l'universite de Geneve 1558–1986* (Geneva: University of Geneva, 1987), 17. For a pre-history of the Genevan Academy, see also William G. Naphy, "The Reformation and the Evolution of Geneva's Schools," in Beat A. Kumin, ed., *Reformations Old and New: Essays on the Socio-Economic Impact of Religious Change, c.1470–1630* (London: Scholar

By the time of Calvin's arrival, city officials yearned for a premier educational institution, but in 1536 most Genevans thought this was a target too ambitious. It is also clear that success in establishing a lasting university did not occur until Calvin set his hand to the educational plow after Geneva became settled in its Protestant identity in the 1550s.

Calvin's Academy, which was adjacent to St. Pierre Cathedral, featured two levels of curricula: one for the public education of Geneva's youth (the college or *schola privata*) and the other a seminary to train ministers (*schola publica*).[4] One should hardly discount the impact that came from the public education of young people, especially in a day when education was normally reserved only for aristocratic scions or for members of Catholic societies. The Academy was begun in 1558,[5] with Calvin and Theodore Beza chairing the theological faculty. A building for the institution was dedicated on June 5, 1559, with 600 people in attendance in St. Pierre Cathedral. Calvin collected money for the school, and many expatriates donated to help its formation. The public school, which had seven grades, enrolled 280 students during its inaugural year, and the Academy's seminary expanded to 162 students in just three years. By Calvin's death in 1564, there were 1,200 students in the college and 300 in the seminary. Both schools, as historians have observed, were tuition-free and "forerunners of modern public education."[6] Few European institutions ever saw such rapid growth.

Press, 1996), 190–93. Until recently, Charles Borgeaud's *Histoire de l'universite de Geneve* (Geneva, 1900) was the standard history.

4. E. William Monter, *Calvin's Geneva* (New York: John Wiley & Sons, 1967), 112. The *schola privata* began classes in the fall of 1558, and the *schola publica* commenced in November of 1558. Marcacci, *Histoire de l'universite de Geneve*, 17.

5. Public records for January 17, 1558, refer to the establishment of the college, with three chairs (theology, philosophy, Greek). Notice was also given commending the college as a worthy recipient of inheritance proceeds. See Henry Martyn Baird, *Theodore Beza: The Counselor of the French Reformation, 1519–1605* (New York: G. P. Putnam's Sons, 1899), 104.

6. See Donald R. Kelley, *Francois Hotman: A Revolutionary's Ordeal* (Princeton: Princeton University Press, 1973), 270.

To accommodate the flood of students, the Academy planned to add—in what would become characteristic of the Calvinistic view of Christian influence in all areas of life—departments of law and medicine. Beza requested prayer for the new medical department as early as 1567, by which time the law school was established. Following the St. Bartholomew's Day massacre (1572), Francis Hotman—and several other leading constitutional scholars—taught at the Genevan law school. The presence of two legal giants, Hotman (from 1573–1578) and Denis Godefroy, gave Calvin's Academy one of the earliest Swiss legal faculties. The medical school, attempted shortly after Calvin's death, was not successfully established until the 1700s.[7] Calvin's Academy became the standard bearer for education in all major fields.

Historically, education, as much as any other single factor, has fostered cultural and political advancement. One of Calvin's most enduring contributions to society—a contribution that also secured the longevity of many of the Calvinistic reforms—was the establishment of the Academy in Geneva. Through his Academy, Calvin also succeeded where others had failed. Worth noting, none of the other major Protestant Reformers are credited with founding a university that would last for centuries, even becoming a sought-after property by some surprising suitors—like Thomas Jefferson.[8]

2. Care for the Poor: The Bourse

Most people do not instantly associate Calvin with sympathy for the poor or indigent. However, a cursory review of his care for orphans, the needy, and displaced refugees in a period of crisis

7. Baird, *Theodore Beza*, 106, 113.

8. For this intriguing story, see my summation in *The Genevan Reformation and the American Founding* (Lanham, MD: Lexington Books, 2003), 2–4. I am indebted to Dr. James H. Hutson for this fascinating anecdote, which he presents in his *The Sister Republics: Switzerland and the United States from 1776 to the Present*, 2nd ed. (Washington, DC: Library of Congress, 1992), 68–76.

not only shows otherwise, but also provides enduring principles for societal aid for the truly needy.

Calvin thought that the church's compassion could best be expressed through its ordained deacons, who represented the epitome of private charity. The challenge for Calvin was to derive practical protocols that would enable proper care for the poor, using the diaconal mechanisms that God had already provided through the church's ministry of mercy.

Jeannine Olson's able historical volume *Calvin and Social Welfare: Deacons and the Bourse Francaise* is an eye-opening study of Calvin's impact on Reformation culture, focusing particularly on the enduring effect of his thought on social welfare through the church's diaconate. In her treatise, Olson noted that, contrary to some modern caricatures, the Reformers worked diligently to shelter refugees and minister to the poor. The Bourse Francaise became a pillar of societal welfare in Geneva;[9] in fact, this mercy ministry may have had nearly as much influence in Calvin's Europe as his theology did in other areas.

The activities of the Bourse were numerous. Its diaconal agents were involved in housing orphans, the elderly, or those who were incapacitated. The Bourse sheltered the sick and dealt with those involved in immoralities. This ecclesiastical institution was a precursor to the voluntary societies of the nineteenth and twentieth centuries in the West. Calvin was so interested in seeing the diaconate flourish that he left part of his family inheritance in his will for the Boys School and for poor immigrants.[10]

The initial design of the Bourse was to appease the suffering of French residents who, while fleeing sectarian persecution in France, settled in Geneva. It has been estimated that in the single decade of 1550 to 1560, some 60,000 refugees passed through Geneva, a number capable of producing significant social stress.

9. Jeannine Olson, *Calvin and Social Welfare: Deacons and the Bourse Francaise* (Cranbury, NJ: Susquehanna University Press, 1989), 11–12.

10. Cited by Geoffrey Bromiley, "The English Reformers and Diaconate," *Service in Christ* (London: Epworth Press, 1966), 113.

The deacons cared for a large range of needs, not wholly dissimilar to the strata of welfare needs in our own society. They provided interim subsidies and job-training as necessary; on occasion, they even provided the necessary tools or supplies so that an able-bodied person could engage in an honest vocation. Within a generation of this welfare work, Calvin's diaconate discovered the need to communicate to recipients the goal that they were to return to work as soon as possible. They also cared for cases of abandonment, supported the terminally ill who, in turn, left their children to be supported, and also included a ministry to widows who often had dependent children and a variety of needs.

Naturally there were theological values buttressing these reforms, and these theological distinctives led to certain practical commitments. View on calling, human inability, the value of work, and the role of the church as a private social safety-net determined how needs were met. Modern leaders might be better off to see what they can learn from the past; in summary, we find the following as principles of Calvin's influential welfare reform:

+ It was only for the truly disadvantaged.
+ Moral prerequisites accompanied assistance.
+ Private or religious charity, not state largesse, was the vehicle for aid.
+ Ordained officers managed and brought accountability.
+ Theological underpinnings were normal.
+ A productive work ethic was sought.
+ Assistance was temporary.
+ History is valuable.

One of Calvin's fellow Reformers, Martin Bucer, went so far as to say of the diaconate that "without it there can be no true communion of saints."[11] In a sermon on 1 Timothy 3:8–10, Calvin

11. Basil Hall, "Diaconia in Martin Butzer," *Service in Christ* (London: Epworth Press, 1966), 94.

himself argued that the early church's compassion should be the measure of our own Christianity: "If we want to be considered Christians and want it to be believed that there is some church among us, this organization must be demonstrated and maintained."[12] Calvin even on one occasion rhetorically asserted, "Do we want to show that there is reformation among us? We must begin at this point, that is, there must be pastors who bear purely the doctrine of salvation, and then deacons who have the care of the poor."[13]

3. Ethics and Interpretation of the Moral Law: The Decalogue

Calvin's interpretation of the Ten Commandments as ethical pillars was widely influential for generations of character development. In his discussion, Calvin argued that this moral law was necessary; for even though man was created in God's image, natural law alone could only assist in pointing toward the right directions. Although acknowledging conscience as a "monitor," still Calvin knew that depravity affected such conscience, and people were "immured in the darkness of error."[14] Thus, mankind was not left to natural law alone, lest it be given over to arrogance, ambition, and a blind self-love. The law, then, was as gracious as it was necessary. Such a fundamentally positive view of God's law would become a distinctive ethical contribution of Calvinism.

The law also shows people how unworthy they are and leads them to distrust human ability. Calvin frequently used phrases like "utter powerlessness" and "utter inability" to make the point that people are dependent on God's revelation if they are to do well. The law is a "perfect rule of righteousness," even though our

12. John Calvin, *Sermons on Timothy and Titus* (Edinburgh: Banner of Truth, 1983), in loc.

13. Ibid., in loc.

14. *Institutes*, 2.8.1.

natural minds are not inclined toward obedience.[15] Calvin noted that the law is full of ramifications, and that it should not be limited to narrow applications. There is always, he wrote, "more in the requirements and prohibitions of the law than is expressed [literally] in words." Each commandment also required its opposite. If one was not to steal, then he also should protect his and others' property. If one was not to lie, then he was to tell the truth. And if one was not to commit adultery, then he should cultivate marital fidelity. Calvin believed that we must reason from the positive command to its opposite in this way: "If this pleases God, its opposite displeases; if that displeases, its opposite pleases; if God commands this, he forbids the opposite; if he forbids that, he commands the opposite."[16] This wide application of the moral law created the basis of an ethical theory that spread throughout the West in time, and it also exhibited a sophistication that was not always present in some theologies.

Calvin believed that the Law had many practical functions—it convinced like a mirror; it restrained like a bridle; and it illumined or aroused us to obedience. However, another chief design of God's law was to guide and remind believers of God's norms.

Calvin's commentary on sexuality (when discussing the seventh commandment) spans less than a thousand words in the *Institutes* but is ever so profound. His discussion of "thou shalt not steal" was rich with texture, calling for a person not only to avoid theft but also to "exert himself honestly to preserve his own" estate.[17] These and other commentaries formed the Protestant work ethic. Similarly, when Calvin spoke of the internal scope of the commandment prohibiting false testimony, he noted that it was "absurd to suppose that God hates the disease of evil-speaking in the tongue, and yet disapproves not of its malignity in the mind."[18] While those expositions may be

15. Ibid., 2.8.5.
16. Ibid., 2.8.8.
17. Ibid., 2.8.45.
18. Ibid., 2.8.48.

brief, they are excellent and so worthy of consulting that most Protestant confessions did just that thereafter. Some of the codifications in various Puritan contexts would follow Calvin's train of thought on the need for and proper use of the law.

Calvinists, then, were not legalists but admirers of the perfections and wisdom of God's law, which they trusted more than themselves. Calvin's followers regarded their own native abilities with such low esteem and God's revealed law with such high esteem that they became the creators and supporters of constitutionalism and law as positive institutions. Moreover, charity was the aim of law, and purity of conscience was the intended result.

4. Freedom of the Church: The Company of Pastors

Calvin labored extensively to permit the church to be the church—and the culture was impacted by a robust, vibrant church. Less than two years after Calvin's arrival in Geneva, he was exiled from the city.[19] The struggle that brought about this result was an important one, involving whether the church and her ministers could follow their own conscience and authority or whether the church would be hindered by state or other hierarchical interference.

Calvin and William Farel (pastoring the Genevan churches of St. Pierre and St. Gervais respectively) declined to offer communion to the feuding citizenry in 1538, lest they heap judgment on themselves.[20] In return, the City Council exiled the two men for insubordination on April 18, 1538. In 1541, however, Calvin was implored to return to Geneva.

19. Henri Heyer, *Guillaume Farel: An Introduction to His Theology*, Blair Reynolds, trans. (Lewiston, NY: The Edwin Mellen Press, 1990), 60.

20. Arthur David Ainsworth, *The Relations between Church and State in the City and Canton of Geneva* (Atlanta, GA: The Stein Printing Company, 1965), 15, reports that the unrest began with a minister denouncing the political government from the pulpit, which led to his arrest.

When he returned, rather than seeking more control for himself over church or civic matters, he sought to regularize a republican form of church government. One of Calvin's demands before returning to Geneva in September 1541 was that a collegial governing body of pastors and church elders from the area be established. When it came time to replace ineffective centralized structures, rather than opting for an institution that strengthened his own hand, this visionary Reformer lobbied for decentralized authority, lodging it with many elected officers instead of with a self-perpetuating elite. He also insisted that the church be free from political interference—separation of jurisdictions, not a yearning for theocratic oppressiveness, helped to solidify the integrity of the church, too—and his 1541 *Ecclesiastical Ordinances* specifically required such a separation.

Calvin and Farel's first priority upon their re-engagement in Geneva was the establishment of the protocols in Calvin's *Ecclesiastical Ordinances*, a procedural manual which prescribed how the city churches would supervise the morals and teaching of its own pastors without hindrance from any other authorities. The priority that Calvin assigned to this work shows how important it was for him that the church be free to carry out its own affairs, unimpeded by the state. The sovereignty of the ministerial council (Consistory)[21] to monitor the faith and practice of the church was codified in these 1541 *Ordinances*. They were later revised in 1561, just prior to Calvin's death, and provided enduring procedures for a free church. Obviously, this arrangement marked a departure from the traditional yoking of political and ecclesiastical influence under Roman Catholic auspices. The Genevan innovation also

---

21. The first Consistory in 1542 was comprised of twelve elders elected annually by the magistrates and nine ministers. The number of ministers had grown to nineteen by 1564. The Consistory met each Thursday to discuss matters of common interest and church discipline. Since Calvin insisted so strongly on this institution after his Strasbourg period, some believe that he imitated the practice of Bucer. Alister McGrath, *A Life of John Calvin: A Study in the Shaping of Western Culture* (Oxford: Basil Blackwell, 1990), 111, 113.

differed slightly from the current practices in Bern and Lausanne, both of which were also Protestant.

In nations or regions where the civil government has ever or often sought to influence the church to change its views, this Calvinistic signature is greatly appreciated. A church free from external, hierarchical, or civil control was a radical and lasting contribution that Calvin made to the modern world. When the church is effective at promoting her God-given virtues, that free church is a powerful influence for society's good.

5. Collegial Governing: The Senate

Calvin also argued long and hard that government should not and could not do everything; it had to be limited in its task and scope. If it was not, it would run aground as in the time of the Hebrew prophet Samuel.

Calvin's sermon on 1 Samuel 8 addresses one of the most widely expounded passages about political thought in Scripture. His 1561 exposition discusses the dangers of monarchy, the need for proper limitation of government, and the place of divine sovereignty over human governments. It is an example of Calvinism at its best, carefully balancing individual liberty and proper government.

Calvin began his sermon on 1 Samuel 8 by asserting that the people of Israel were, even at the last minute prior to electing a king, still free to change their minds; such freedom rendered the kingship optional.[22] Then Samuel warned them "that the king who will reign over them will take their sons for his own purposes and will cause much plundering and robbery." Calvin preached that "there are limits prescribed by God to

22. Quotations in this section are taken from Douglas Kelly's translation of Calvin's sermon on 1 Samuel 8 in Charles Raynal and John Leith, eds., *Calvin Studies Colloquium* (Davidson, NC: Davidson College Presbyterian Church, 1982).

their [kings'] power, within which they ought to be satisfied: namely, to work for the common good and to govern and direct the people in truest fairness and justice; not to be puffed up with their own importance, but to remember that they also are subjects of God."

Calvin's calls to submit to the governor were not without limit. God established magistrates properly "for the use of the people and the benefit of the republic." Accordingly, kings also had charters to satisfy: "They are not to undertake war rashly, nor ambitiously to increase their wealth; nor are they to govern their subjects on the basis of personal opinion or lust for whatever they want." Kings had authority only insofar as they met the conditions of God's covenant. Accordingly, Calvin proclaimed from the pulpit of St. Pierre, "[S]ubjects are under the authority of kings; but at the same time, kings must care about the public welfare so they can discharge the duties prescribed to them by God with good counsel and mature deliberation."

The republican-type plan suggested by Jethro (Moses' father-in-law in Exodus 18) appears as an innovation that did not originate in the mind of man, thought Calvin. Other commentators, ranging from Aquinas and Machiavelli to Althusius and Ponet, viewed Jethro's advice as a pristine example of federalism or republicanism. Commenting on a similar passage in Deuteronomy 1:14–16, Calvin stated:

> Hence it more plainly appears that those who were to preside in judgment were not appointed only by the will of Moses, but elected by the votes of the people. And this is the most desirable kind of liberty, that we should not be compelled to obey every person who may be tyrannically put over our heads; but which allows of election, so that no one should rule except he be approved by us. And this is further confirmed in the next verse, wherein Moses recounts that he awaited the consent of the people, and that nothing was attempted which did not please them all.

Thus, Calvin viewed Exodus 18 as a representative republican form.[23] Geneva's smallest Council of Twenty-Five was also known as the Senate.

This Genevan beacon, whose sermonic ideas later reached the shores of America, enumerated from the Samuel narrative the ways in which kings abuse their power, and he distinguished a tyrant from a legitimate prince in these words: "a tyrant rules only by his own will and lust, whereas legitimate magistrates rule by counsel and by reason so as to determine how to bring about the greatest public welfare and benefit." Calvin decried the oppressive custom of magistrates' "taking part in the plundering to enrich themselves off the poor."

The character of Calvinism is exhibited in this (and other) sermons that advocated limited government. Calvin was correct that individual responsibility was a good and necessary speed bump to check a government taking over more than it should. With this idea, he altered the trajectory of governance.

6. Decentralized Politics: The Republic

One of the procedural safeguards of the 1543 civic reform—a hallmark of the Calvinistic governing ethos—was that the various branches of local government (councils) could no longer act unilaterally; henceforth, at least two councils were required to approve measures before ratification.[24] This early republican mechanism, which prevented consolidation of all governmental power into a single council, predated Mon-

23. For more support of this thesis, see my "Government by Moses and One Greater Than Moses," in *Election Day Sermons* (Oak Ridge, TN: Kuyper Institute, 1996).

24. In 1542 the General Council adopted this proviso: "Nothing should be put before the Council of Two Hundred that has not been dealt with in the Narrow Council, nor before the General Council before having been dealt with in the Narrow Council as well as the Two Hundred" (translation by Kim McMahan). Monter, *Calvin's Geneva*, 72.

tesquieu's separation of powers doctrine by two centuries—a Calvinistic contribution that is not always recognized. The driving rationale for this dispersed authority was a simple but scriptural idea: even the best of leaders could think blindly and selfishly, so they needed a format for mutual correction and accountability. This kind of thinking, already incorporated into Geneva's ecclesiastical sphere (imbedded in the 1541 *Ecclesiastical Ordinances*) and essentially derived from biblical sources, anticipated many later instances of political federalism. The structure of Genevan presbyterianism began to influence Genevan civil politics; in turn, that also furthered the separation of powers and provided protection from oligarchy. The result was a far more open and stable society than previously, and Calvin's orientation toward the practical is obvious in these areas.

The process of Genevan elections itself was a mirror of Calvin's view of human nature and the role of the state. In one of the earliest organized democratic traditions, Calvin's fellow citizens elected four new syndics (commissioners) from a slate of eight for an annual term. Various levels of councils were then elected by the citizens.

This Calvin-shaped polity, which appeared to be either liberal or daringly democratic for its day, provided checks and balances, separation of powers, election by the residents, and other elements of the federal structure that would later be copied as one of Geneva's finest exports. Additional features of federalism, including an early appellate system, were developed by the late 1540s. Not only was Calvin's Geneva religious,[25] but she also sought the assent of the governed to a degree not previously seen, leading the world to new and stable forms of republicanism. At the very least, one should

---

25. In early Massachusetts, church attendance was sanctioned. Absenting oneself from church in Reformed Geneva drew a fine. E. William Monter, *Studies in Genevan Government, 1536–1605* (Geneva: Droz, 1964), 79.

acknowledge "the rather striking correlation, both in time and in place, between the spread of Calvinist Protestantism and the rise of democracy."[26]

In keeping with the teachings of Calvin,[27] elected governors perceived themselves as having a duty to God, one that compelled them to serve the public good and avoid pursuing personal benefit. This notion of selfless political duty owed much of its staying power to Calvin, and it soon became an integral feature of Genevan public culture. Municipal officials were not full-time salaried employees in the time of Calvin, and the combination of checks and balances between the various councils required government to be streamlined and simple. Political offices in Geneva, in contrast with medieval and some modern customs, were not profitable for office holders. Service in such offices was even avoided by some, requiring the threat of a fine if a citizen refused to serve after election.[28]

Geneva became the chief laboratory for the implementation of many of Calvin's republican ideas. As such, the city's local political model yields hints about the character of Calvinism, complete with its tendency to limit government. Features such as limited terms, balance of powers, citizen nullification, interpositional magistracies, and accountability were at the heart of New World governments—which further amplified Calvinism to other generations and locales.

Many ideas that began with Calvin's reformation in Geneva and later became part of the fabric of America were cultivated and crossbred in the seventeenth-century. Customs now taken for granted, like freedom of speech, assembly, and dissent, were

26. Robert M. Kingdon, *Calvin and Calvinism: Sources of Democracy* (Lexington, MA: D. C. Heath and Company, 1970), vii.

27. Monter observed that Calvin did not so much purpose to instruct the existing magistrates "as to show others what magistrates are and for what end God has appointed them." Monter, *Studies in Genevan Government*, 58.

28. Ibid., 57.

extended as Calvin's Dutch, British, and Scottish disciples refined these ideas.

7. Parity among All Professions: The Doctrine of Vocation

Another of the culture-shaping aspects of Calvin's thought was his emphasis on the sacredness of ordinary vocations. Before Calvin and the Protestant Reformation, the doctrine of vocation or calling was thought to be exclusively for the clergy. However, Calvin's view of work as having inherent dignity given by our Creator elevated all disciplines and lawful vocations to the status of holy callings. One could, after Calvin, be called to medicine, law, or education just as a clergyman was called to serve the church.

Calvin's call for hard work did not necessarily equate success or prosperity with divine blessing. His views, though, did have a persistent tendency of ennobling various areas of human calling and labor. Business, commerce, and industry were all elevated by Calvin's principles, and those who adhered to these became leaders of modern enterprise.

Max Weber and others are correct to identify that Calvinism dignified work and callings of many kinds. Calvin taught that any area of work—farming, teaching, governing, business—could be a valid calling from God, every bit as sacred as serving as a minister. This was a radical change in worldview, which would ultimately alter many economies, cultures, and human lives.

The formation of the Genevan Academy under Calvin called for general education (not only in religious studies), and it provided for studies in law, medicine, history, and education. Calvin and other Reformers helped retire the sacred/secular distinction. He sought to educate Genevans in a new way of viewing human labor, namely, that a person could serve God and glorify him in any area of labor. Calvin counseled with many leaders, entrepreneurs, printers, and merchants in his time, and he did not revile any lawful calling. The character of Calvinism ennobles all good work. Despite its emphasis on the hereafter, Calvinism called its adherents to be leaders in all fields of human endeavor in the here and now.

Calvin's commentary on the fourth commandment as stated in Exodus 20 underscores the dignity of work also. Just as God commanded people to rest on the seventh day, so the Lord expected them to work on the other six days. Work was vital for all people made in God's image, and thus, for Calvin, all callings were important. Calvin's doctrine of work and rest was widely popularized.

Calvin agreed with Paul in the New Testament that whether we eat or drink, we do all to the glory of God. That is why the great post-Reformation composer Johann Sebastian Bach signed each of his original scores with the initials "SDG." Those letters stood for the Latin phrase *soli deo Gloria* ("to God alone be the glory"). That organist knew the character of Calvinism and applied it to his craft. Some of the finest Christians in history have also applied the Lordship of Christ to their own vocations and served as leaders in various fields for the glory of God. It is no accident that Rembrandt (art), Milton (poetry), Althusius (political theory), Grotius (international law), Adam Smith (economics), and many others refined their callings while operating from a Calvinistic worldview. Calvin's thought seemed to unleash development and progress in numerous vocations of life.

8. Economics and Profit: The Invisible Hand

Of interest to historians, both those sympathetic and those unsympathetic to Calvin, is the fact that whatever the Reformer was doing during this time transformed Geneva into a visible and bustling forum for economic development. With a growing intellectual ferment, evidenced by the founding of Calvin's Academy and the presence of modern financial institutions (e.g., a Medici bank), Geneva became an ideal center for perfecting and exporting reform.[29]

Wherever Calvinism spread, so did a love for free markets and capitalism. If one valid measurement of leadership is its impact on its immediate environment, one might well compare the socio-economic difference in Geneva *before* and *after* Calvin. This difference may be noted by comparing three key occupational segments. Prior to Calvin's immigration (1536), Geneva had 50 merchants, 3 printers, and few, if any, nobles. By the late 1550s, Geneva was home to 180 merchants, 113 printers and publishers, and at least 70 aristocratic refugees who claimed nobility.[30]

However, it is certainly erroneous to think, like Max Weber in his *The Protestant Ethic and the Spirit of Capitalism* (1905), that Calvinists equated material success with a sign of being the elect. To rebut that idea, one may simply consult Calvin's teaching on the eighth commandment, which forbade stealing. Calvin interpreted that the holding and protecting of personal property was by implication perfectly normal. In fact, that commandment, properly understood, forbade the greedy coveting of what others have, and

29. Several studies detail Calvin's Geneva. Among the best are: E. William Monter, *Calvin's Geneva* (New York: John Wiley & Sons, 1967); Alastair Duke, Gillian Lewis, and Andrew Pettegree, eds., *Calvinism in Europe, 1540–1610: A Collection of Documents* (Manchester, UK: Manchester University Press, 1988); J. T. McNeill, "John Calvin on Civil Government," in George L. Hunt, ed., *Calvinism and the Political Order* (Philadelphia: Westminster Press, 1965), 22–45; William A. Dunning, *A History of Political Theories: From Luther to Montesquieu* (New York: Macmillan, 1919), 26–33; W. Fred Graham, *The Constructive Revolutionary: John Calvin, His Socio-Economic Impact* (Richmond, VA: John Knox Press, 1975); William G. Naphy, *Calvin and the Consolidation of the Genevan Reformation* (Manchester, UK: Manchester University Press, 1994). Two recent biographies also add to our understanding: William Bouwsma's *John Calvin: A Sixteenth-Century Portrait* (New York: Oxford University Press, 1988) and Alister McGrath, *A Life of John Calvin* (Oxford: Basil Blackwell, 1990).

30. Monter's numbers, of course, may be challenged. It is possible that records were kept better after 1536, which could explain some of the rise of the merchant class (*Calvin's Geneva*, 5). However, even should that be established, the astronomic rise of printers and nobility is certain. Nobles, mainly from France, fled to Geneva because adhering to Protestantism at home could have meant their deaths.

required every person to "exert himself honestly in preserving his own [property]." Calvin warned believers not to squander what God has providentially given and also to care for their neighbors' well-being. He also saw this commandment as calling for contentment with "our own lot," and that

> we study to acquire nothing but honest and lawful gain; if we long not to grow rich by injustice, nor to plunder our neighbor of his goods . . . if we hasten not to heap up wealth cruelly wrung from the blood of others; if we do not . . . with excessive eagerness scrape together whatever may glut our avarice or meet our prodigality. On the other hand, let it be our constant aim faithfully to lend our counsel and aid to all so as to assist them in retaining their property.[31]

The common but mistaken caricature of Calvin as a crass capitalist should be contrasted with the prayer he suggested using before beginning work and which is included in the 1562 Genevan Catechism. In that prayer, he led the people in asking God to bless their labor, noting that if God did not bless it, "nothing goes well or can prosper." He prayed for the Holy Spirit to aid workers in this calling so that they would work "without any fraud or deception, and so that we shall have regard more to follow their ordinances than to satisfy our appetite to make ourselves rich." Along with this, Calvin prayed that workers would also care for the indigent and that the prosperous would not become conceited. He prayed that God would diminish prosperity if he knew that the people needed a dose of poverty to return them to their senses. Far from being callous toward the less fortunate, Calvin prayed that workers would "not fall into mistrust," would "wait patiently" on God to provide, and would "rest with entire assurance in thy pure goodness."[32]

31. *Institutes*, 2.8.46.
32. Duke, Lewis, and Pettegree, *Calvinism in Europe*, 34.

He also asserted that any endeavor that ceased to have charity as its aim was diseased at its very root. Elsewhere, Calvin warned that luxury could incite great problems and produce "great carelessness as to virtue." Moreover, he warned against "eagerly contend[ing] for riches and honors, trusting in our own dexterity and assiduity, or leaning on the favor of men, or confiding in any empty imagination of fortune; but [we] should always have respect to the Lord." Lest Calvin be misunderstood, he also called for a "curb to be laid on us" to restrain "a too eager desire of becoming rich, or an ambitious striving after honor."[33] The prosperity ethic that followed his time in Geneva is one of the wide-ranging but misconstrued effects of his thought and practice. But he also advocated reliance on God—not wealth!

9. Music in the Vernacular: The Psalter

One of Calvin's early initiatives was to translate music designed for use in public worship into the language of the day. Realizing that what people sing in a holy context has enduring impact on how they act, Calvin wanted worship—in all its aspects—to be intelligible. Shortly after his settling in Geneva, he urged a talented musician, Clement Marot, to translate the psalms into mid-sixteenth-century French. Calvin wanted everyone who participated in worship, not only the clergy, to be able to understand and reiterate the truths of Scripture—this time in poetic structure. His democratizing of holy song and other elements of worship made parishioners participants in the divine liturgy; simultaneously, it also boosted the endeavors of artists.

Hymns and songs powerfully lodged distinct ideas in the popular mind, especially when aided by reading the Bible in the common language and hearing sermons that could be understood by the masses. The singing of psalms afforded Protestants the occasion to

33. *Institutes*, 2.8.45.

confess their beliefs, while some anti-Protestants went so far as to view the singing of psalms as an inherently subversive act![34]

Marot never completed his translation and arrangement of the psalms, but Calvin's disciple Theodore Beza was as committed, if not more so, to this project which would both alter the nature of Protestant worship and further engrain scriptural teachings into what eventually became the Puritan mind. Beza even sponsored a hymn-writing contest shortly after Calvin's death in his attempt to match the poetry of the Psalter with singable tunes.

Perhaps the largest single printing venture of the sixteenth century, Beza's French translation of the psalms into metrical form, went to press in Geneva's old town.[35] This Psalter, which became the international songbook of expansionistic Calvinism, went through numerous editions (27,400 copies were printed in 1562 alone). Stanford Reid notes that to a greater degree than "all the fine theological reasoning, both the catechism and the Psalter entered into the very warp and weft of the humblest members' lives. For this the credit must largely go to the first pastor of Geneva."[36]

Besides the various Psalters, other vehicles that aided in the importing of Calvinism to the West were the Geneva Bible and Beza's *New Testament Annotations*. These inspired readers ranging from Shakespeare (who, in his plays composed during the

34. W. Stanford Reid, "The Battle Hymns of the Lord: Calvinist Psalmody of the Sixteenth Century," *Sixteenth Century Journal*, vol. 2, no. 1 (1971): 43, 45. Reid comments: "Whether one thinks of the fourteen martyrs of Meaux who sang the 79th Psalm, the five scholars of Lausanne in Lyon who sang Psalm 9, or others who turned to other parts of the Psalter as they went to their deaths, one can see how in the last great struggle of faith, the psalms indeed were true battle hymns" (46). These Psalms, once engrained, fit "every occasion and form of resistance" (idem).

35. Monter, *Calvin's Geneva*, 181.

36. Reid, "The Battle Hymns of the Lord," 36–54, speaks of the psalms as the battle hymns of "one of the earliest modern resistance movements." Reid also describes Calvin's view of church music as a *via media* between Luther's liberal embrace of contemporary music and Zwingli's elimination of music at the Grossmunster.

1590s, quoted from the Geneva Bible)[37] to American colonists and featured "scores of marginal notes on covenant, vocation . . . deposition of kings, the supremacy of God's Word [over human tradition], and the duty of orderly resistance to tyranny."[38] Beza and Marot's hymnbook of metrical psalms, which became surprisingly popular, paved the way for acceptance of other ideas championed by the enormously influential Beza.[39] Accordingly, art was elevated and became useful for cultural progress.

When Puritan settlers colonized North America, one of the consistent best sellers of the day was the Bay Psalter, a thinly disguised revision of Calvin's Psalter. Calvin's disciples knew that the faith that sings powerful truths will also pass those truths on to future generations, and worship music set in the vernacular was a strong step in that direction.

10. The Power of Publishing Ideas: The Genevan Presses

If Martin Luther seized on the potential of the printing press, Calvin and his followers elevated the use of the press to an art form. With the rise of the Gutenberg press, Reformers seized the new media with a vengeance to multiply their thought and action plans. Perhaps no first generation Reformer seized the moment quite like John Calvin. Expressing his thoughts with clarity and regularity was part of his life.

37. See David L. Edwards, *Christian England: From the Reformation to the Eighteenth Century* (Grand Rapids: Eerdmans, 1983), 146. In "A Translation Fit for a King," *Christianity Today* (October 22, 2001), David Neff argues how powerfully the translation of the Bible aided the flow of liberty. "Logically," Neff notes, "it is a fairly short step from the biblical language of liberty to the secular politics of liberty." For more, see this article online at: http://www.christianitytoday.com/ct/2001/013/6.36.html.

38. Kingdon, *Calvin and Calvinism*, 40.

39. Herbert D. Foster, *Collected Papers of Herbert D. Foster* (privately printed, 1929), 93.

The ability of Calvin and his followers to defend his views rapidly in print magnified the lasting impact of his thought.[40] The number of books published in Geneva rose from 3 volumes in 1536 to 28 in 1554 and to 48 by 1561. In the five years prior to Calvin's death, a stunning average of 38 volumes per year were printed (a ten-fold increase in 25 years). The average dropped to 20 per year after his death.[41] By 1563, there were at least 34 presses in the city, many manned by immigrants.[42] Shortly after Calvin's death, one contemporary wrote: "The printed works flooding into the country could not be stopped by legal prohibition. The more edicts issued by the courts, the more the booklets and papers increased."[43]

Geneva also developed an extensive and efficient literary distribution system. A childhood friend of Calvin, Laurent de Normandie (who later became mayor of Noyon), developed a network of distributors who took Genevan Calvinist publications into France and other parts of Europe. Many of the books were designed to be small for quick hiding within clothing, if need be.[44] Thousands of contraband books were spread throughout Europe during Calvin's time, and several distributors of literature became Protestant martyrs.[45]

40. McGrath contrasts Calvin's success with that of Zurich Reformer Vadian, and identifies Calvin's "extensive publishing programme" as one of the differences. McGrath, *A Life of John Calvin*, 124–126.

41. Monter, *Calvin's Geneva*, 179.

42. Robert Kingdon explains that the number was likely more since some were co-opted by others. In 1562, neighbors complained that paper mills were running round the clock. Robert M. Kingdon, *Geneva and the Coming Wars of Religion in France, 1555–1563* (Geneva: Librairie Droz, 1956), 94. Jean Crespin even contracted to purchase bales of paper from outside Geneva (95).

43. William G. Naphy, ed., *Documents on the Continental Reformation* (New York: St. Martin's Press, 1996), 87.

44. Monter, *Calvin's Geneva*, 182. Robert Kingdon notes that the books were so well circulated that as early as 1560 the Cardinal of Lorraine had successfully collected 22 pamphlets that had criticized him. Kingdon, *Geneva and the Coming Wars of Religion in France*, 103. Another historian in 1561 reported the spread to Paris of Beza's Psalter, catechisms, and popular Christian books, "all well bound in red and black calf skin, some well gilded" (103).

45. Monter, *Calvin's Geneva*, 182.

So successful was Calvin's city at spreading the message in print that all books published in Geneva were banned in France beginning in 1551. Calvin's *Institutes of the Christian Religion* (along with at least nine of his other writings) had been officially banned in France since 1542, but that could not halt the circulation of his books. As a result, Geneva was identified as a subversive center because of its publishing; and the 1551 Edict of Chateaubriand forbade, among other things, importing or circulating Genevan books.[46] Distributing such works for sale could incur secular punishment. However, many books still filtered across porous European borders. Some shrewd printers, unwilling to be thwarted by state censorship, responded cleverly by employing type fonts that were commonly used by French printers and publishing their works under fictitious addresses.[47] This new medium and its energized distribution pipeline allowed Calvin's message to transcend Geneva's geographical limitations.

Calvin's thought spread throughout Europe and sailed over the Atlantic with various colonists, cropping up frequently in sermons and pamphlets in various colonies. If English sermons in the seventeenth century were still referencing Calvin's *Institutes* as a robust source for opposing governmental abuse, American colonial sermons conveyed his sentiments even more. Wrote Dartmouth historian Herbert Foster,

> Probably no other theological work was so widely read and so influential from the Reformation to the American Revolution. . . . In England [it] was considered "the best and perfectest system of divinity" by both Anglican and Puritan until [Archbishop William] Laud's supremacy in the 1630s. Oxford undergraduates were required to read Calvin's *Institutes* and his Catechism in 1578.[48]

46. Duke, Lewis, and Pettegree, eds., *Calvinism in Europe*, 57.
47. McGrath, *A Life of John Calvin*, 12. See also E. Droz, "Fausses adresses typographiques," *Bulletin of Historical Research* 23 (1961): 380–86, 572–74.
48. Kingdon, *Calvin and Calvinism*, 37. The sermon referred to by Foster is a 1663 sermon by British minister Robert South, who referred to Calvin as "the great mufti of Geneva." *Collected Papers of Herbert D. Foster*, 116.

"Most colonial libraries seem to contain some work by Calvin," and "scarcely a colonial list of books from New Hampshire to South Carolina appears to lack books written by Calvinists."[49]

Even the Scottish philosopher David Hume, a fan of neither Knox nor Calvin, admitted that "the republican ideas of the origin of power from the people were at that time [about 1607] esteemed as Puritan novelties."[50] Calvin's ideas, then, took on a life of their own and were eagerly emulated by many others. This success was due in no small measure to the printing press and Calvin's wise employment of the latest technology. A strong case can be made that the most determinative religion at the time was Calvinism or one of its offshoots. Long after his death in 1564, Calvin would live on through his writings, which are still widely available today, and continue to mentor many generations of disciples.

Epilogue

The Calvinist view of liberty, wherever it spread, gave citizens confidence and protections. Within a century, the American

49. Kingdon, *Calvin and Calvinism*, 37. Other historians argue that the Puritanism of New England was "patterned after the Westminster Catechism and embodied the type of Calvinistic thought current in all of New England at that time." See Peter De Jong, *The Covenant Idea in New England Theology, 1620–1847* (Grand Rapids: Eerdmans, 1945), 85. Foster, *Collected Papers*, 79, lists the numerous Americans who owned copies of Calvin's *Institutes*. Patricia Bonomi has also firmly established that the majority of seventeenth-century Americans followed "some form of Puritan Calvinism, which itself was divided into a number of factions." See Patricia U. Bonomi, *Under the Cope of Heaven: Religion, Society, and Politics in Colonial America* (New York: Oxford University Press, 1986), 14.

50. David Hume, *The History of England* (Philadelphia: Lewis and Baker, 1810), 5:469, cited in George Buchanan, *De Jure Regni Apud Scotos*, trans. Charles Flinn Arrowood, 17, available online at www.contra-mundum.org/books/jure/jure-introduction.pdf.

colonies would exhibit these Calvinistic distinctives. Not incidentally one of the first colonial law-codes was named "The Massachusetts Body of Liberties." So close were law and liberty that Calvin's disciples customarily associated law codes with tables of liberties. The reason was that a proper understanding of liberty is essential for any successful venture, whether it is business, civic, or religious. Calvin had seen an oppression of liberties—both in Paris as Protestants were persecuted and in the eyes of the many Roman Catholic refugees who arrived so regularly at Geneva's walls—and he formed his view of liberties based on God's Word and also in a fashion that avoided misuses of it.

Few thinkers from this period or from a past period have as much future relevance as Calvin. Calvin set forth both the positive necessity for well-ordered government and the limitations of its scope. His Reformed theology compelled government to be limited to the role of servant of the people; his political insights helped restrain the Leviathan. Today, when individuals frequently act as if centralized government agencies can provide lasting solutions to a wide range of social and individual problems, Calvinistic realism is one of the few substantial intellectual traditions that cogently warns against the twin dangers of utopianism and the threat of expansive governmental power.

Of all theologies, Calvinism has made the most significant contribution to democracy. One summary of political Calvinism reduced Calvin's ideas to five points that may be of continuing validity. Herbert Foster noted the following as hallmarks of Calvin's political legacy,[51] and these permeate the cultural contributions noted above:

51. Foster, *Collected Papers*, 163–74. I have summarized the five points of political Calvinism slightly differently, referring to: Depravity as a perennial human variable to be accommodated; Accountability for leaders provided via a *collegium*; Republicanism as the preferred form of government; Constitutionalism needed to restrain both the rulers and the ruled; and Limited government, beginning with

1. The absolute sovereignty of God entailed that universal human rights (or Beza's "fundamental law") should be protected and must not be surrendered to the whim of tyranny.
2. These fundamental laws, which were always compatible with God's law, are the basis of whatever public liberties we enjoy.
3. Mutual covenants, as taught by Beza, Hotman, and the *Vindiciae*, between rulers and God and between rulers and subjects were binding and necessary.
4. As Ponet, Knox, and Goodman taught, the sovereignty of the people flows logically from the mutual obligations of the covenants above.
5. The representatives of the people, not the people themselves, are the first line of defense against tyranny.[52]

At least an elementary grasp of Calvin is essential to any well-informed self-understanding of Western democracy—indeed, for modernity itself. Unfortunately, many remain unaware of the signal contribution that the leadership of Calvin has made to open societies. We may even credit Calvin's Reformation with aiding the spread of participatory democracy. Even if this heritage no longer holds a place of honor in our textbooks or in our public tradition, we owe our Calvinistic forefathers a large debt of gratitude for their efforts to establish limited government and personal liberty grounded in virtue. A single man with heart aflame changed the world.

American Supreme Court Justice Antonin Scalia once estimated the paramount political accomplishment of the millennium

the family as foundational. The resulting mnemonic device, DARCL, though not as convenient as TULIP, seems a more apt summary if placed in the context of the political writings of Calvin's disciples.

52. Ibid., 174. Besides Calvin, this idea was reiterated in Buchanan, Beza, Peter Martyr, Althusius, Hotman, Daneau, *Vindiciae*, Ponet, William the Silent, and others. Ibid.

as law established by elected representatives instead of by the king or his experts. Scalia's candidate for the *fin-de-millénaire* award in late 1999 was

> the principle that laws should be made not by a ruler, or his ministers, or his appointed judges, but by representatives of the people. This principle of democratic self-government was virtually unheard of in the feudal world that existed at the beginning of the millennium. . . . So thoroughly has this principle swept the board that even many countries that in fact do not observe it pretend to do so, going through the motions of sham, unopposed elections.[53]

Scalia continued:

> We Americans have become so used to democracy that it seems to us the natural order of things. Of course it is not. During almost all of recorded human history, the overwhelming majority of mankind has been governed by rulers determined by heredity, or selected by a powerful aristocracy, or imposed through sheer force of arms. Kings and emperors have been always with us; presidents (or their equivalent) have been very rare.[54]

However, it should be noted from the highlights above that Justice Scalia is describing the kind of republicanism pioneered by Calvin and his disciples—a republicanism grounded in the eternal truth of morally ordered liberty.

Even during the twentieth century, intellectuals certainly remained aware of Calvin. In fact, in the words of contemporary theologian Douglas Kelly, Calvin's legacy continues and is "perhaps the stronger and deeper for the very fact that its roots are largely unperceived." Large segments of political

---

53. Antonin Scalia, "The Millennium That Was: How Democracy Swept the World," *The Wall Street Journal*, September 7, 1999, A24.
54. Ibid.

thought have often embraced such forward-looking Calvinistic concepts as respecting fixed limits on governing power and permitting people the rights to resist oppression with little awareness of the genesis of these ideas.[55] Calvin's original formulation of these ideas was eventually "amplified, systematized, and widely diffused in Western civilization. . . . Thus modified, it would prevail across half of the world for nearly half a millennium."[56]

Calvin should certainly be acknowledged for his overall contribution to the legacy of freedom and openness in democratic societies. It is undeniable that he had a large influence on the American founding fathers, who had absorbed much more Calvinism, particularly in their views of the nature of man and the need for limited government, than some realize.

John Calvin was much more than a theologian, and his influence extended far beyond churches.[57] Calvin and his disciples, when measured by this new millennium, will probably be seen to have made more lasting contributions than Karl Marx, Napoleon Bonaparte, Albert Einstein, Bill Gates, or Henry Ford. Calvin inspired the cultural changes that gave rise to the political philosophy of the American founders, a truly extraordinary event in world history. Founding fathers, such as George Washington, James Madison, Samuel and John Adams, Patrick Henry, and Thomas Jefferson[58] stood on the

55. Douglas Kelly, *The Emergence of Liberty in the Modern World* (Phillipsburg, NJ: P&R Publishing, 1992), 4, 27.

56. Ibid., 32.

57. Some of the foregoing work was also contained in my dissertation, "The Calvinistic Political Tradition, 1530–1790: The Rise, Development, and Dissemination of Genevan Political Culture to the Founders of America through Theological Exemplars" (Whitefield Theological Seminary, April 2002).

58. A recent article further corroborates Jefferson's ease with religion. See "What Would Jefferson Do?" *The Wall Street Journal*, March 9, 2001, D26. That editorial contains a finding by Kevin Hasson: "The Framers did not share the suspicion that religion is some sort of allergen in the body politic. Quite the contrary, they welcomed public expression of faith as a normal part

shoulders of some of history's greatest philosophers, not the least of whom was a pastor from Geneva who lived nearly five hundred years ago. That he is still commemorated as a significant leader half a millennium after his birth indicates the robust character of his thought and the sturdiness of a legacy that will last for generations to come.

With the above signatures of Calvin's cultural contributions in mind, perhaps a brief sketch of his life will be of interest.

---

of cultural life." It is also noted that in Jefferson's day the Treasury Building was used for a Presbyterian communion, Episcopal services were held in the War Office and, as the Library of Congress exhibition states, "the Gospel was also preached in the Supreme Court chambers." That America today does not know its own history is a reflection of the larger revisionism that portrays the churches, synagogues, and mosques that criss-cross the country not as bulwarks of freedom but as incipient threats to the American way of life. The editorial concludes by suggesting that if future Supreme Court justices are hostile to the free expression of religion, "they'll have to do it without Jefferson."

JOHN CALVIN: A LIFE
WORTH KNOWING

I t is admittedly difficult for most people today to relate to
John Calvin or to his times. He lived half a millennium ago
(b. 1509), but in terms of experience and culture he may
seem closer to the Paleolithic period than to our own decade
or century. Thus, it is understandable that in order for us to
relate to him, he must be personalized and contextualized.
That is a fair challenge, and this abbreviated biography seeks
to ease that burden and close that gap. Building such a bridge
to the past can help us see that this Genevan theologian can
still serve as a helpful exemplar for many different fields of
human endeavor.[1]

1. Classic biographies of Calvin include: Theodore Beza, *Life of John Calvin*,
contained in John Calvin, *Tracts and Treatises on the Reformation of the Church*
(Grand Rapids: Eerdmans, 1958); T. H. L. Parker, *A Biography of Calvin* (Phila-
delphia: Westminster John Knox, 2007); William J. Bouwsma, *John Calvin: A
Sixteenth-Century Portrait* (New York: Oxford University Press, 1988); Alister
McGrath, *A Life of John Calvin* (Cambridge, MA: Basil Blackwell Ltd., 1990);
and Emile Doumergue, *The Character of Calvinism: The Man, His System, The
Church, The State* (1923; repr. Neuilly [Seine]: La Cause, 1931).

In Calvin's day, Europe was a quilt of various tribes, family alliances, and fiefdoms. The most centralized power was the Roman Catholic Church, which sought to hold Christendom together. The city of Geneva, which became important as the primary staging area of Calvin's activities, was not removed from these greater trends. Whether priests or governors realized it, a Reformation was about to commence in the early decades of the sixteenth century, and human society would change irrevocably through the decisive leadership of men like this academic who preferred to shun the spotlight.

Calvin stood at the onset of modernity, and his ideas and actions would change history forever. Others—today, mainly forgotten—have previously recognized the influence of Calvin. The highly respected nineteenth-century Harvard historian George Bancroft was one of many who earlier asserted that Calvin's ideas buttressed liberty's cause. Bancroft and others noted the influence of this thought on the development of various freedoms in Western Europe and America.[2] Writing in the middle of the nineteenth century, Bancroft even credited many of the public freedoms in the West as being chiefly transmitted through Calvin's disciples, the Puritans. Moreover, Bancroft traced the living legacy of Calvin among the Plymouth pilgrims, the Huguenot settlers of South Carolina, and the Dutch colonists in Manhattan, concluding: "He that will not honor the memory and respect the influence of Calvin knows but little of the origin of American liberty."[3]

Bancroft esteemed Calvin as one of the premier republican pioneers, at one point writing, "The fanatic for Calvinism was a fanatic for liberty; and, in the moral warfare for freedom, his creed was his most faithful counselor and his never-failing support. The Puritans . . . planted . . . the undy-

2. See Philip Schaff, *History of the Christian Church*, 8 vols. (1910; repr. Grand Rapids: Eerdmans, 1979), 8:264.
3. Ibid., 8:522.

ing principles of democratic liberty."[4] During the nineteenth century, appreciation of the societal impact of Calvin was not limited solely to American scholars. The world-renowned German historian Leopold von Ranke, for example, reached the similar conclusion that "John Calvin was virtually the founder of America."[5]

Calvin's Life

Little is known about John Calvin's mother, Jeanne la France of Cambrai, due to her early death; his father was a dominant presence in his early life and education.

Calvin was born on July 10, 1509,[6] in Noyon, a small town about 50 miles northeast of Paris in Picardy, France. He was the middle son in a family with five children—three sons and two daughters. His father, Gerard, was an administrative assistant in the nearby cathedral complex, and his mother died when Calvin was only five.[7] His first biographer, his friend and colleague, Professor Theodore Beza, later described Calvin as "of middle stature, sallow features, and whose piercing eye and animated looks announced a mind of no common sagacity."[8]

Calvin's father enrolled him in the College de Montaigu in Paris in 1521, intending for him to enter the priesthood. While at that Parisian college, Calvin studied rhetoric, logic, and arts—common topics for the day—and received a classical education. He was also influenced by the work of the

4. Cited in Robert M. Kingdon, *Calvin and Calvinism: Sources of Democracy* (Lexington, MA: D. C. Heath and Company, 1970), xiii. The original citation is George Bancroft, *History of the United States of America* (Boston, 1853), 1:464.

5. Cited in Kingdon, *Calvin and Calvinism*, 7.

6. Beza idiosyncratically dates Calvin's birth at July 27, 1509. See Theodore Beza, *Life of John Calvin* 1:lvii.

7. Bouwsma, *John Calvin*, 9.

8. Cited in J. H. Merle D'Aubigne, *The History of the Reformation of the Sixteenth Century* (New York: American Tract Society, 1848), 3:474.

leading Roman Catholic progressive, John Major[9]—a tower-ing intellect—and Peter of Spain.[10] The major theological assumptions during his education at Paris included a hearty concurrence with Augustine on man's nature, a pessimistic view of humanity flowing from the Fall and original sin, and rejection of salvation by human merit.[11] According to one historian, "Calvin's powers of reasoning and analysis may be traced to his rigorous training" under such Parisian masters. He also could not avoid the deluge of intellectual currents, especially the inchoate Protestantism, swirling through Paris at the time.

His instruction included training in three classic languages: Latin, Greek (learned from Melchior Wolmar at Orleans, to whom Calvin dedicated his commentary on 2 Corinthians), and Hebrew. Calvin's "humanist" education[12] included enrollments at key education institutions near Paris[13] (Orleans, Bourges, Basle) and familiarization with other learning centers of the day. He was exposed to the thought of Erasmus, Le Fevre, Wol-mar, and Francois Rabelais, a veritable *Who's Who* of Western European education for his day. Calvin would later complete in Paris the equivalent of a master's degree in an education that ranked with or surpassed those of Cambridge or Oxford

9. Some historians see a common pedagogical strain, insofar as it is likely that Calvin, Knox, and Buchanan were all former students of John Major. J. T. McNeill, "Calvinism and European Politics in Historical Perspective," in George L. Hunt, ed., *Calvinism and the Political Order* (Philadelphia: Westminster Press, 1965), 15. Douglas Kelly sees Major's *History of Great Britain* as especially influential on Knox and Buchanan.

10. McGrath, *A Life of John Calvin*, 34. For a recent evaluation of the place of Calvin, see also Alister McGrath, "Calvin and the Christian Calling," *First Things* 94 (June/July 1999): 31–35.

11. McGrath, *A Life of John Calvin*, 45.

12. The humanism of the day emphasized the classics. *Ad fontes*, or "back to the sources," became the rallying cry of the new educational model of Calvin's time.

13. McGrath notes that an inscription on the façade of the Bibliotheque Sainte-Genevieve in Paris lists Calvin, along with Erasmus and others, as an intellectual leader. McGrath, *A Life of John Calvin*, 21.

at the time. A free market of new ideas and Protestantism (originally thought of as "Lutheranism") surged in Paris while Calvin was a student there.

His education was a bold new one that sought to appreciate the classics of the past and also accorded less reverence to the traditions of Roman Catholicism. Calvin was a modern scholar who understood the role of criticism in arriving at truth. His first published work, a commentary on Seneca's *De Clementia* (1532), affirmed the radical notion that "[T]he prince is not above the laws, but the laws above the prince."[14] Later, his published works would concentrate on a wide array of theological subjects.

Calvin's father played a dominant role in his early education at Paris, and Gerard eventually persuaded his son to train for the legal profession, which he considered a surer path to wealth than the priesthood. Since France was a monarchy, and the king was above the law, it was too much cognitive dissonance to house a law school in Paris—as if the king might ever be subject to a constitution; thus, France's leading law school was located in Orleans and not Paris. From 1528 to 1533, Calvin studied law in Bourges and Orleans,[15] a preparation that would assist him in later endeavors, including laying the foundation for subsequent political ideas. He was later licensed to practice law, and his legal training ultimately aided him as he mentored Geneva's developing republic.

Whether the guiding hand was his father's or that of the Father of Providence, Calvin was exposed to the best teachers of the day. His education would serve him well all his life, and the opportunity to study under these master teachers was of great value.

If it had been left up to his own wishes, John Calvin would have continued to pursue a comfortable academic career. He did

14. Harro Hopfl, *The Christian Polity of John Calvin* (Cambridge: Cambridge University Press, 1982), 16.
15. Beza called Calvin's teacher at Orleans, Peter de L'Etoile, "the keenest jurisconsult of all the doctors of France." Cited in Douglas Kelly, *The Emergence of Liberty in the Modern World* (Phillipsburg, NJ: P&R Publishing, 1992), 8.

not intend either to serve as a pastor or to work in Geneva, but God had other plans for him.

Calvin's only autobiographical account of his spiritual conversion appears in the 1557 Preface to his *Commentary on Psalms*.[16] He did not wear his conversion on his sleeve but took many opportunities to practice what he preached. From Calvin's own testimony, he rarely saw himself as breaking new ground, and he described the Book of Psalms as "An Anatomy of all the parts of the Soul." No sterile scholastic, as he has often been maligned, Calvin claimed that "there is not an emotion of which any one can be conscious that is not here [in the Psalms] represented as in a mirror." All the "lurking places" of the heart were illumined in these devotional poems.

He prefaced his spiritual testimony by stating his appreciation for other Reformed teachers of the time, particularly praising Martin Bucer and Wolfgang Musculus. He was happy to acknowledge his indebtedness to others, once praising Luther in this fashion: "It was a great miracle of God that Luther and those who worked with him at the beginning in restoring the pure truth were able to emerge from it little by little."[17] Although Calvin would differ significantly with Luther on several issues, he retained a lifelong admiration for Luther's work and saw himself as building on a shared foundation. Calvin stated that, should Doctor Martin call him a devil, he would "nevertheless hold him in such honor [and] acknowledge him to be a distinguished servant of God."[18] While exiled in Strasbourg (1538–41), Calvin also forged a strong relationship with Luther's understudy, Philip Melanchthon.

16. All citations from Calvin's self-testimony about his spiritual conversion are taken from his Preface to his commentary on Psalms in *Calvin's Commentaries*, vol. 4 (repr. Grand Rapid: Baker Book House, 1979).

17. *Traite des scandales* (1560), in Albert-Marie Schmidt, ed., *Oeuvres de Jean Calvin* (Paris, 1934), 2:251, cited in Bouwsma, *John Calvin*, 11.

18. Cited in Bouwsma, *John Calvin*, 18.

In his clearest spiritual autobiography, Calvin likened himself to David, as one who had been taken from a pastoral venue and thrust into a position of public responsibility. He reviewed for his readers how his father had destined him for the priesthood, how Gerard considered the legal profession more lucrative, and had enrolled young Calvin in legal studies. Calvin reflected on his early education, noting that even there divine providence was guiding him, despite his earthly father's urgings toward law for ignoble reasons.

John Calvin's religious upbringing (he later called it "superstitious"), was not abandoned easily. Even though he was plunged into a profound spiritual abyss, according to his own account, Calvin was found by God, who used a sudden conversion to "subdue and bring my mind to a teachable frame, which was more hardened in such matters than might have been expected from one at my early period in life." Apparently Calvin continued traditional Roman Catholic practices until his conversion in 1533–34.

After this "sudden conversion," the Parisian student found himself "inflamed with an intense desire," and he fervently pursued Protestant teachings. After a year of diligent study (so intense perhaps because Protestantism was new and also because Calvin studied under some of the finest teachers in the pristine movement), he was surprised that numerous people began to treat him like an expert on these matters. He humbly viewed himself as unpolished, bashful, retiring, and preferring seclusion. Yet, like the author of the Psalms, he sensed that he was inevitably being thrust into the role of a public leader. Instead of successfully living in scholarly quiescence, all his retreats became public debating forums. He wrote: "In short, while my one great object was to live in seclusion without being known, God so led me about through different turnings and changes that he never permitted me to rest in any place, until in spite of my natural disposition, he brought me forth to public notice."

In the early sixteenth century, Paris had become a hotbed of reform movements that had been particularly influenced by the Italian Reformers Savonarola and Peter Martyr. However, in the fall of 1533, French monarch Francis I cracked down on the burgeoning Protestantism, which was causing considerable commotion in Paris.

The immediate cause of this crackdown was the installation of Nicholas Cop, a Protestant sympathizer, to lead the university. Some theorize that Calvin, perhaps, lent his literary expertise to help draft Cop's inaugural address. True or not, Calvin himself believed it necessary to leave Paris immediately after Cop's delivery of the address. His escape from Paris was none too soon, as police seized his personal papers within hours of his departure.[19]

Although not as dramatic as Luther's conversion,[20] Calvin's awakening was nonetheless absolute: he left Paris a committed Protestant in 1533. Recent scholars have rediscovered the "suddenness" of his conversion, the term Calvin himself preferred. Calvin entirely severed his relationship with the Roman Catholic Church by spring 1534.[21] Later he would rendezvous in Basle with his mentor, Nicholas Cop, the ousted rector of the University of Paris, in Basle, where both men made their Protestant sympathies public. Much of the 1534–35 period was devoted to searching for an environment where the Reformation would be welcomed. Calvin had contacts with Geneva as early as 1535. While in Basle, he observed the development of the Reformation, monitoring both the ongoing debates and the resulting attacks on Protestants.[22] After 1536, Calvin no longer considered himself a Parisian.

19. McGrath, *A Life of John Calvin*, 15.
20. It must be remembered that Calvin was more private than Luther, less colorful, and in general timid about autobiography. In addition there are certainly gaps in our knowledge about him.
21. McGrath, *A Life of John Calvin*, 73.
22. Ibid., 76.

Calvin recounts how he left his native France and wandered in Germany in search of obscurity (at various times, Calvin had to resort to using aliases, including Charles d'Espeville, Martianus Lucanius, Carolus Passelius, Alcuin, Depercan, and Calpurnius),[23] only to settle temporarily in Basle. It was at Basle that he learned of numerous deaths of French Protestants who had been burnt alive, which provoked passionate disapproval from Calvin and the other German-speaking Protestants "whose indignation was kindled against such tyranny." Calvin apparently developed an antipathy to state tyranny from an early age.

Calvin wanted to avoid the fray, nevertheless. His own spiritual pilgrimage indicates that he resolved to devote himself to quiet scholarly obscurity, until William Farel detained him in Geneva, "not so much by counsel and exhortation as by a dreadful imprecation, which I felt to be as if God had from heaven laid his mighty hand upon me to arrest me." The myths about Farel's imprecation are numerous. Yet, even though the exact words are lost, it is clear that Farel applied some fiery threats to Calvin's conscience.

Since the direct highway to Strasbourg was dangerous, Calvin sought another path, intending to spend no more than a single night in Geneva. He expected Geneva to be relatively safe in 1536, crediting the partial triumph of Protestantism there largely to Peter Viret—a fellow Reformer from Lausanne who would remain a close friend for years. Although the conflicts in Geneva were by no means over—"the city was divided into unholy and dangerous factions"—Calvin nevertheless thought it safer than the Strasbourg route. While Calvin expected only a short stay in Geneva, someone conveyed his itinerary to William Farel, whom Calvin described as burning "with an extraordinary zeal to advance the gospel." Farel then "strained every nerve to detain" Calvin. After Calvin initially rejected Farel's summons, Farel resorted to calling down curses

23. Schaff, *History of the Christian Church*, 8:322.

on Calvin's plans for a life of tranquil academic pursuits. These curses terrorized Calvin to the point that he acceded to Farel's demand, despite his natural timidity and reticence.

Thus Calvin, the reluctant and shy Reformer, began his work in Geneva with the unostentatious title of Lecturer on the Holy Scriptures in the Church of Geneva. That city and the world would not be the same thereafter.

The psychological self-portrait seen in his commentary on the Psalms is contrary to the malicious profiles compiled later by biased or hostile critics. Calvin's disciple and eventual biographer, Theodore Beza, noted the following traits of Calvin: he was modest, temperate, thin (he normally ate only one daily meal because of an intestinal ailment), possessed an astonishing memory, was unusually attentive, and of clear judgment and counsel. Beza recorded how Calvin "despised mere eloquence, and was sparing in the use of words. No theologian of this period wrote more purely.... With regard to his manners, although nature had formed him for gravity, yet ... there was no man who was more pleasant."[24] Moreover, Beza was not surprised that "one endowed with so great and so many virtues should have had numerous enemies." The Reformer's disciple even had the foresight to deny that Calvin "reigned at Geneva, both in church and state, so as to supplant the ordinary tribunals"[25]—an early hint about Calvin's belief in the separation of jurisdictions.

But even with such a promising beginning, Calvin would learn—as many other leaders have—that success is seldom easy or rapid. Calvin would soon suffer a setback that might have terminated lesser leaders, but his consuming passion for eternal truths enabled him to persevere. His genuine spirituality would be needed to sustain him through difficulties as soon as his short-lived honeymoon in Geneva was over.

24. Beza, *Life of John Calvin*, 1:cxxxvi.
25. Ibid., 1:cxxxviii.

Calvin settled in Geneva in July 1536. By the fall of 1536, the Genevans initiated their new political culture with a large public debate and the presentation of a Confession of Faith written by Calvin.[26] The four syndics (chief assemblymen) elected in February 1537 were all Farel sympathizers, and reorganization progressed steadily until a 1538 electoral backlash.

By this time, the combined powers of certain patrician families, residual Catholic sympathies, and internal political pressure within Geneva led to Calvin and Farel's exile to Strasbourg.[27] New Genevan elections took effect in early 1538, and the new officials were less zealous for the Reformation; indeed, some openly opposed the combined efforts of Calvin and Farel.[28] Following the change of administrations, Calvin and many Genevans found themselves at odds with certain factions and leaders within the city. Due to the extraordinary infighting among the townsfolk at the time, Calvin and Farel declined to offer communion to the feuding citizenry, lest they heap judgment on themselves.[29] In return, the City Council exiled them for insubordination two days later, on April 18, 1538—less than two years after Calvin's arrival.[30] Some leaders would have considered this a crushing blow.

26. McGrath, *A Life of John Calvin*, 96–97.

27. William Naphy suggests that part of the 1538 disruption was due to the fact that Genevans did not wish to offend their protector-ally Bern by adopting a confession of faith that may have been viewed as a threat to Bern. Thus, some felt that Calvin's reform was moving too rapidly or could alienate the Bernese, on whom some Genevans thought their freedom depended. William G. Naphy, *Calvin and the Consolidation of the Genevan Reformation* (Manchester, UK: Manchester University Press, 1994), 28.

28. Henri Heyer, *Guillaume Farel: An Introduction to His Theology*, Blair Reynolds, trans. (Lewiston, NY: The Edwin Mellen Press, 1990), 59.

29. Arthur David Ainsworth, *The Relations between Church and State in the City and Canton of Geneva* (Atlanta, GA: The Stein Printing Company, 1965), 15, reports that the unrest began with a minister denouncing the political government from the pulpit, which led to his arrest.

30. Heyer, *Guillaume Farel*, 60.

Beza, however, in his biography of Calvin, viewed this exile to Strasbourg as part of "Divine providence," enabling Calvin to train for greater effectiveness while employing his gifts to strengthen another city. It also allowed for the "overthrowing [of] those seditious persons . . . to purge the city of Geneva of much pollution." Accordingly, "Satan was disappointed" and "saw Calvin received elsewhere, and, as a substitute for the Genevan Church, another Church forthwith erected."[31]

After this initial brush with defeat, Calvin once again resolved to retreat from the public eye, only later to be urged to return to Geneva by the esteemed Martin Bucer in tones very similar to Farel's earlier summons. Calvin's humility, which is often underappreciated, is evident from many parts of the written record. In the conclusion of his only autobiographical explanation of his conversion, he refers to his wishing to "avoid celebrity" while inexorably being pushed to the fore of "Imperial assemblies, where, willing or unwilling, I was under the necessity of appearing before the eyes of many."

Calvin's three years in Strasbourg, however, would be essential for his future. His exile ended in 1541 when he returned to Geneva "contrary to [his] desire and inclination." What motivated him to return to the place where he had been so rudely treated only a few years earlier? "The welfare of this church . . . lay so near my heart," he stated, "that for its sake I would not have hesitated to lay down my life." Competing with his natural diffidence, the weight of "solemn and conscientious duty" was greater than his personal comfort. Still, it was with considerable grief, tears, anxiety, and distress (not to mention "a remarkable act of social pragmatism and religious realism"[32]) that he returned to Geneva.

Calvin's biographer sheds light on the Reformer's trepidation about returning to Geneva in 1541. After "the Lord had deter-

---

31. Beza, *Life of John Calvin*, 1:lvii, lxxi–lxxii.
32. McGrath, *A Life of John Calvin*, 86.

mined to take pity on the Church of Geneva," all four of the anti-Calvin elected officials had either been removed, executed for civil crimes, or condemned. The city "being thus rid of its filth and froth," wrote Beza, "began to long for its Farel and its Calvin." Beza explained that, since neither Farel (now in Neuchatel) nor Calvin wanted to return, it took arm-twisting from leaders in Zurich to convince them to return. Beza also noted that Calvin's reasons why he did not wish to return included his aversion to conflict and his sense that his ministry in the Church of Strasbourg was going well. Moreover, Martin Bucer and others initially declared that they had great objections to losing Calvin's services in Strasbourg.[33]

One of Calvin's demands before returning was that a collegial governing body of pastors and church elders from the area be established.[34] When it came time to replace ineffective centralized structures, rather than opting for an institution that strengthened his own hand, this visionary Reformer lobbied for decentralized authority lodged with many officers. He also insisted that the church be free from political interference— separation of jurisdictions helped to solidify the integrity of the church, too—and his 1541 *Ecclesiastical Ordinances* specifically required such a separation.

These clues indicate that moving Geneva into the Protestant column did not come easily, quickly, or without repeated accusations against the Reformers.

Calvin's sojourn in Strasbourg from 1538 to 1541, however, proved providential, as he later claimed. It was in Strasbourg, a city that had already traveled further down the path of Reformation than had Geneva, that Calvin saw the full potential of Reformed religion and politics. Under the powerful example of such leading educators of the Reformation as Johann Sturm (1507–89) and

33. Beza, *Life of John Calvin*, 1:lxxv.
34. Ibid., 1:lxxvi.

Martin Bucer, Calvin received sound mentoring there. He accompanied Bucer on diplomatic missions, taught in Sturm's freshly minted Academy that became a model for Geneva's own, and observed a harmonious relationship between church and state.[35] Calvin also pastored 400–500 French Protestant refugees.[36] Just prior to returning to Geneva, he became a citizen of Strasbourg and met a widow, Idelette De Bure, who became his wife. Calvin's only son with Idelette (Jacques, born on July 28, 1542) died in infancy, and he inherited Idelette's two daughters by a previous marriage, becoming their only surviving parent after Idelette's death in 1549.

When his wife died, Calvin faced an unparalleled grief. His letters to Farel and Viret reveal both his faith in God and his love for Idelette. This was a grief observed, and those watching developed admiration. He paid high tribute to Idelette, extolling her as an excellent companion in exile, sorrow, or death.

In Calvin's case, his abiding confidence in the providence of God fueled his passions even during exile and defeat. By using his time well during his Strasbourg residency, he not only added to his portfolio of experience, but he was also used of the Lord in that period. When it came to an end, he was more prepared—precisely because of this providential detour—to lead the Reformation from Geneva. Calvin is a superb historical example of a leader who rose, then fell, but recovered from his defeats and learned to use the time as well as he could in the interim.

In 1541, after a three-year absence from Geneva and following the demise of some of their political opponents, Calvin and Farel[37] returned triumphantly to Geneva in what one historian

---

35. McGrath, *A Life of John Calvin*, 101.

36. Schaff, *History of the Christian Church*, 8:368.

37. At the time, Farel was settled in Neuchatel and was reluctant to return. He persuaded Calvin of the need. On September 13, 1541, Calvin re-entered Geneva. McGrath, *A Life of John Calvin*, 103.

called a miracle "beyond human conception."[38] The chief official of Geneva, Louis Dufour, delivered an invitation co-signed by all three elected Councils of Geneva imploring Calvin to return; Dufour even traveled to Strasbourg to woo the exiled Calvin (who, at that time, was participating in a colloquy at Worms).[39] The citizens of the Lac Leman region urged Calvin to resume his unfinished work, and the council forwarded to him moving expenses and an honorarium. In addition, they promised to pay Calvin a salary higher than the syndics' own if he returned! Later, in 1543, they also provided him with a home near St. Pierre Church.

Calvin's and Farel's first priority upon their re-engagement was the establishment of the protocols in Calvin's *Ecclesiastical Ordinances*, a procedural manual which prescribed how the Genevan church would supervise the affairs of its pastors and the congregations within its jurisdiction. Calvin manifested his strong intention to secure freedom for the church to control her own activities apart from state interference. The sovereignty of the ministerial council (Consistory) to monitor the faith and practice of the church was codified in these 1541 *Ordinances*. With the publication of the *Ordinances*, "Geneva created a unique Christian commonwealth whereby church and state cooperated in preserving religion as the key to their new identity. Geneva was not the first city to develop a radically Reformed theology and polity. Much of Calvin's theological thinking was indebted to his early contact with Martin Bucer and his residence in Strasbourg."[40] Strasbourg may have been "the New Jerusalem" and the cradle of the Reformation's new understanding on government, but Geneva, with its innovative reforms and political distillation of Protestant theology

38. Ronald S. Wallace, *Calvin, Geneva and the Reformation* (Edinburgh: Scottish Academic Press, 1988), 41.

39. Schaff, *History of the Christian Church*, 8:431.

40. John B. Roney and Martin I. Klauber, eds., *The Identity of Geneva: The Christian Commonwealth, 1564–1864* (Westport, CT: Greenwood Press, 1998), 3.

under Calvin's guidance, would eventually surpass Strasbourg and become known as the "Protestant Rome."

Despite the rise of commerce, however, the story of Calvin's leadership and impact on the region was not primarily economic. The translation of the Reformed faith into practice is witnessed by the creation of tell-tale social structures that emerged from the leadership of Farel and Calvin. A hospital was launched in 1535, and a fund for French refugees (*Bourse Francaise*) was established by church deacons in 1541. Calvin's Academy was founded in 1558. Eventually, thousands of refugees (mainly French, English, and Italian) came to Geneva for shelter; and many later returned to their own lands with fresh ideas about the relationship of citizens to government.[41]

Historian William Naphy views the rise of a competent class of elders and senators as instrumental in establishing Calvinism as a lasting political force in Geneva and Europe. Leading their procession, Naphy writes, "stood Calvin, a figure increasingly famous throughout Europe; as Calvin increased in importance, Geneva gained international prominence. This new-found fame may well have aided Geneva in fending off the intentions of neighbouring states desirous of controlling the city."[42] Moreover, as the electoral base stabilized in Geneva after the 1540s, along with solidarity among its church leaders, Calvin was able to expand the role of the Genevan ministers both at home and abroad. He was also sufficiently popular and insulated enough from internal opposition to devote the final decade of his life to implementing his social and political reforms. The longevity of Calvin's influence is decidedly different after the return from his exile. What made that influence enduring was, to the surprise of many planners, a private, charitable institution—the church.

41. See also Jeannine E. Olson's "Social Welfare and the Transformation of Polity in Geneva," in Roney and Klauber, *The Identity of Geneva*, 155–68.
42. Naphy, *Calvin and the Consolidation of the Genevan Reformation*, 224.

While Calvin's accomplishments have had lasting influence in many sectors, it is important to recognize an oft-ignored truism about his work: his reforms began in the church and only then radiated outward. As a leader, Calvin practiced what he preached. A consistency of ideals, both in church and state, permeated his thought and action. He was prudent enough to realize that the best way to reform the culture was indirectly, that is, to first reform the church.

When Calvin returned to St. Pierre Cathedral in 1541, he unceremoniously but symbolically resumed his pulpit activity by expounding the Scriptures at the exact verse where he left off prior to his exile. Several days earlier, Calvin had consulted with the Small Council, the real political powerhouse of the day, and encouraged its members to make important reforms. They were so willing to help him in the Reformation of Geneva that they not only approved his proposals to revise the protocols for church order, but they also appointed him to a committee to design a constitution for the Republic of Geneva.[43] The drafts of the constitution indicate that Calvin paid close attention to the minute details of administrative matters and municipal functions, and he made some suggestions for judicial reform.[44] Philip Schaff recorded that Calvin was awarded a cask of old wine as payment for his efforts in revising the city constitution, and that "[m]any of his regulations continued in legal force down to the eighteenth century." Calvin's legal training at Orleans would prove valuable over the course of his life. Occasionally, he was thus called on to divert some of his attention away from church matters in order to assist in this constitutional role or other civic matters.

43. Monter, *Calvin's Geneva*, 72. The 1541 *Ecclesiastical Ordinances* were approved by the Genevan magistrates. Ibid., 127.
44. Schaff, *History of the Christian Church*, 8:464. Schaff also notes here that a later revision of Genevan law codes was undertaken in 1560 in consultation with Germain Colladon.

Recalling that Calvin lived in what might be termed a pre-information age, he would have faced the challenge of finding ways to convey his ideas in widespread fashion. The earliest and broadest method of disseminating Calvin's thought to his contemporaries was through preaching, a decidedly oral medium. This method, which would surely be discounted by most cultural critics today, proved to be greatly beneficial to the Reformation. Calvin spoke to the masses in clear and forceful language, and with regularity he instructed and reached the leading minds of his day.

Contrary to the stereotype that Calvin was a dry or uninteresting pedant, his sermons actually attracted large and consistent audiences. By the mid–1550s, one eyewitness reported that most Genevans, "even the hypocrites," heard these Calvinistic sermons.[45] Preaching might be thought of as the mass communication of the time, and Genevans received a considerable portion of their information from the regular hearing of sermons. During most of Calvin's tenure, sermons were preached daily from all four of Geneva's churches. Stressing simplicity and clarity, Calvin's preaching was ideally designed to persuade the masses and to shape their expectations. In one such exhortation just before a citywide election, Calvin warned about civic dangers threatening the city and called on the listeners to "think carefully and to take God as our president and governor in our elections, and to make our choice with a pure conscience without regard to anything except the honor and glory of God in the security and defense of this republic."[46] His preaching was pervasive, and one of Theodore Beza's 1561 letters to William Farel claimed that over one thousand people heard Calvin's lectures on a daily basis—a considerable accomplishment for the day.[47]

45. Monter, *Calvin's Geneva*, 99.
46. Cited in Duke, Lewis, and Pettegree, *Calvinism in Europe*, 48.
47. See Henry Martyn Baird, *Theodore Beza: The Counselor of the French Reformation, 1519–1605* (New York: G. P. Putnam's Sons, 1899), 200.

Calvin worked at reforming on numerous fronts, not with a coercive and dictatorial spirit but by discourse, persuasion, and forceful rhetoric. One modern study recognizes the role that Calvin's preaching played in interpreting his significance. William Naphy provides examples of how Calvin confronted even the elected officials in his congregation and concludes that Calvin's preaching was at times direct, confrontational, and "politically informed." One 1552 sermon so irritated the Council that they inquired just why Calvin spoke of the Senators and other civil rulers as "arguing against God," "mocking him," "rejecting all the Holy Scriptures [to] vomit forth their blasphemies as supreme decrees," and as "gargoyle monkeys [who] have become so proud."[48] Calvin's rhetoric was certainly not so academic or technical as to elude his audience.

Calvin preached regularly in Geneva and Strasbourg, and his sermons provide rich amplification of his thought, which might otherwise be considered arid if his leadership were evaluated apart from these homilies. Whether he intended to shape culture as much as he eventually did or not, Calvin knew the value of communication that was practical in orientation.

Although Calvin enjoyed preaching *extempore*, his adherents quickly realized the value of recording his expositions. In 1549, mainly at the encouragement of French refugees in Geneva, a recording secretary was appointed to take down Calvin's sermons in writing. These sermons, which were later either lost or sold by the pound for scrap paper following the French Revolution, eventually yielded dozens of volumes in manuscript form—a prolific achievement considering that Calvin had so many other duties in addition to preaching.

During his final residence in Geneva, Calvin regularly preached expositions in the three Sunday services. By 1549, these messages were so popular that they were increased to

48. Naphy, *Calvin and the Consolidation of the Genevan Reformation*, 160.

daily expositions. Calvin's rotation allowed him to preach twice on Sunday and every day in alternating weeks. On average, Calvin thus prepared 20 sermons per month, normally drawing on New Testament texts on Sunday mornings, Old Testament texts during the week, and the Psalms on Sunday afternoons. His fertile mind could not be limited only to writing. Calvin preached 200 sermons on Deuteronomy, 159 on Job, 110 on 1 Corinthians, and 43 on Galatians—each of these being intellectual achievements in its own right. By these free and spirited orations, the common man was enlightened and equipped to carry on the ideas of reform for a long time. Optimizing one medium would only inspire Calvin to employ other means of mass communication as well.

His pioneering work to establish the Academy in Geneva also ensured that Calvin's ideas would survive beyond his own generation. Through the Academy he further succeeded in educating the masses, as well as in training generations of pastors and civic leaders. Both his school and its students would perpetuate the notions expounded in his sermons and writings. By the time of Calvin's death in 1564, there were 1,200 students in the college and 300 in the seminary.

Moreover, the Academy provided excellent education for internationals. This Academy always had a large number of immigrant students. By 1691, French students constituted 40 percent of the student body, while French-speaking Swiss were 25 percent. Only 8.3 percent of the students were Genevan. Enrollment crested near the time of Beza's death, with over 60 graduates per year, and then declined to about 50 per year by 1665 and continued downward to about 20 per year throughout most of the eighteenth century.

A recent study points out that many of the French immigrants who supported the *Bourse Francais* were also the main financial contributors to Calvin's Academy. Thus, an immigrant constituency may have had more lasting impact than previous studies have recognized.[49] This clearly illustrates the fact that Calvin was happy to cooperate with others who were not necessarily long-standing citizens of Geneva.

From 1560 onward, the Genevan Academy also doubled as the ministerial training ground for France and other international centers. According to William Bouwsma, the institution emphasized the trilingual approach fostered by Erasmus:

> Its students were first thoroughly grounded in Latin grammar and rhetoric by the study of Virgil, Cicero, and other classical authors, and in the fourth year they began Greek. They learned history from Livy and Xenophon and dialectic from the arguments of Cicero rather than from medieval textbooks. . . . Calvin's ideal for both pastors and secular rulers resembled Quintilian's generally educated orator, the ideal of humanist educators everywhere.[50]

This training prepared numerous students for professional service, including vocations in law, medicine, politics, and education, as well as the ministry.

Calvin's Academy became the standard bearer for education in all major fields. Three days each week, professors in Hebrew, Greek, and the Arts would give two-hour-long lectures in a morning and an afternoon session; the alternating days would have a one-hour lecture.[51] In time, scholars from Paris and Lausanne flocked to this excellent educational center. Those original students would graduate and lend their hands to drafting influential confessions of faith, serving as political advisors in Scotland, Germany, France, Holland, and England, and teaching at other leading universities. After education at Calvin's Academy, for example, Thomas Bodley returned to

49. See ibid., 142.
50. See Bouwsma, *John Calvin*, 14–15.
51. See Duke, Lewis, and Pettegree, *Calvinism in Europe*, 218.

Oxford and established the Bodleian Library, perhaps the finest research library in the world. His action followed Calvin's educational mission.

Moreover, the Academy exported missionaries. The Genevan church sent over 100 missionaries to France, Brazil, Italy, Holland, and England before 1562.[52] Many of these, including pastors from Geneva and Lausanne, went underground, hid in safe houses, and reappeared in French cities to minister from time to time.[53] Geneva became an energy source for reform, acting at times like the best of resistance movements. Its influence in Europe, England, and Scotland was enormous.[54]

The later history of this educational institution is a noble one as well. As early as 1708, Jean Robert Chouet called for a transition from the Academy to a "university."[55] Numerous chairs of science were added in the 1700s, while the once-stalwart theological faculty began to tend toward rationalism. The school, however, was still called the "Academy" in the 1750s, and many patrician children received an excellent education at the Academy throughout the eighteenth century. It was first known as a "University" in 1798 and was moved to its present location in 1868.

Publishing was an opportunity to take intellectual property and convert it into action treatises for international audiences. The printing industry in Geneva during Calvin's rise to prominence is a story in itself, one that proved crucial for the longevity of Calvin's work. One recent study states: "No description of the international

52. Kingdon lists Thomas Cartwright as a missionary, along with thirteen students from the Genevan Academy, seven other teachers, and seven Genevan pastors between 1564 and 1572. See Kingdon, *Geneva and the Consolidation of the French Protestant Movement*, 203–8. See also Monter, *Calvin's Geneva*, 135.

53. McGrath, *A Life of John Calvin*, 183.

54. The Marian Exiles, for example, were Protestants who fled England during the reign of Queen ("Bloody") Mary, when she attempted to reverse the emergence of Calvinism in that country.

55. Marco Marcacci, *Histoire de L'Universite de Geneve 1558–1986* (Geneva: University of Geneva, 1987), 42.

efforts of the Reform can omit to mention the contributions of the printer and scholar Robert Estienne, the printer and martyrologist Jean Crespin . . . or for that matter the lifelong and deliberate use of publication as a weapon on the part of Calvin and Theodore de Beze."[56] Robert Estienne printed French editions by Calvin's disciples Beza, Hotman, and Viret from Geneva. Jean Crispin, a groomsman at Beza's secret marriage,[57] published popular devotional material; moreover, a wide array of educational material was produced for the burgeoning Academy. Bibles and theological texts flew off Genevan printing presses.

The ability to defend the views of Calvin rapidly in print magnified the lasting impact of his thought.[58] During Calvin's tenure in Geneva, the number of published works grew dramatically. Shortly after Calvin's death, one contemporary wrote: "The printed works flooding into the country could not be stopped by legal prohibition. The more edicts issued by the courts, the more the booklets and papers increased."[59]

The content of publications in Calvin's day was also taken seriously, and efforts were made to ensure that truth was committed to ink. In 1560, a commission on printing was established to coordinate the efforts of the various publishers within Geneva's walls. This three-member commission included Beza and Jean Bude. The area ministerial association (the Company of Pastors) had a strong voice in what was printed, and every manuscript published in Geneva first had to survive Beza's scrutiny.[60] Not

56. Duke, Lewis, and Pettegree, *Calvinism in Europe*, 201.

57. Schaff, *History of the Christian Church*, 8:851.

58. McGrath, *A Life of John Calvin*, 124–26, contrasts Calvin's success with that of the Zurich Reformer, Vadian, and identifies Calvin's "extensive publishing programme" as one of the differences.

59. William G. Naphy, ed., *Documents on the Continental Reformation* (New York: St. Martin's Press, 1996), 87.

60. Robert M. Kingdon, *Geneva and the Coming Wars of Religion in France, 1555–1563* (Geneva: Librairie Droz, 1956), 97. This may explain why Calvinism's publishing headquarters were Genevan shops. Yet, Kingdon avoids the theocratic association by

unpredictably, of the forty-eight Genevan publications in 1561, thirteen were by Calvin, seven by Beza, and five by Viret. Of the thirty-six works published in 1562, over one-third (thirteen) were by Calvin.[61] This leader's ideas thus received a literary megaphone. The new medium of printing and its energized distribution pipeline allowed Calvin's message to transcend Geneva's geographical limitations.

Silk, wine, books, and political and religious ideas became the main exports of Geneva during and following Calvin's tenure. Ultimately, thousands of refugees from all over Europe fled to Geneva, a city that was becoming an international host for freedom of movement, publishing, assembly, and ideas. Moreover, once Geneva's democratic transformation was completed, she did not turn back—thanks to Calvin's work and efforts.

Calvin's Friendships

One defender of Calvin noted that it would be impossible for a man to be so dearly loved at his death if he had been a monster all his life. Not only was Calvin praised at his death, but his many friends had embraced similar ideas and sought to carry them on.[62]

A study of the letters of Calvin reveals a pattern of friendship and collegiality. Calvin certainly did not view himself as the only individual involved in these matters of reform. One such study is *The Humanness of John Calvin* by Richard Stauffer.[63] For "the other side of the story," one should consult this small work. In the

---

noting that "Censorship was the chief duty of the Commission." Even some of Calvin's friends were fined, and some printers had to cease operations (98).

61. Kingdon, *Geneva and the Coming Wars of Religion in France*, 101.

62. This section is taken from my *A Heart Promptly Offered: The Revolutionary Leadership of John Calvin* (Nashville, TN: Cumberland House Books, 2006), 171–76.

63. Richard Stauffer, *The Humanness of John Calvin* (Nashville: Abingdon Press, 1971).

foreword to that monograph, leading Calvin scholar J. T. McNeill chronicled how he had been led to question the "hearsay" about Calvin. As McNeill read Calvin's letters, contrary to the many urban legends that he had heard, he found that Calvin was vividly humane, associated with rich and poor alike, and exhibited a sturdy loyalty to friends. McNeill found the real Calvin to be gentle, warm, tender, generous, and hospitable. Richard Stauffer documents the "calumny" that Calvin has received from his enemies and also how he has "been misunderstood and misinterpreted by his great-grandchildren."[64]

Another historian noted that no other Reformer generated more personal loyalty than Calvin. Emile Doumergue[65] put it this way: "There were few men who developed as many friendships as he and who knew how to retain not only the admiration, but also the personal affection of these friends."[66] Abel Lefranc expressed the same sentiment this way: "The friendships which he inspired . . . among his teachers as well as among his colleagues, are strong enough testimonies to the fact that he knew how to combine with his serious and intense commitment to work, an affability and graciousness which won every one over to him."[67]

64. Ibid., 19.

65. Emile Doumergue wrote a 1923 French work entitled *The Character of Calvinism: The Man, His System, the Church, the State* (1923; repr. Neuilly [Seine]: La Cause, 1931). Doumergue there highlighted the following as distinguishing attributes, among others, of Calvin's character: vivacity, joyishness, affection (Fr. *mignardise*, preciousness), nobility, and a concern to pitch his written style for common understanding. At one point (55), Doumergue notes, "Le style c'est l'homme." Doumergue also credited Calvinism with the "exaltation of the individual" and attributed to it "the perfection of truth" (131). He also viewed the very fabric of the church under Calvin's reforms as epitomizing these three aspects of Calvin's own character: the church was a (1) constitutional, (2) representative, and (3) democratic society (141–42). Correspondingly, Doumergue noted that the state had a similar character, distinguishing, nonetheless, the state as "elective (not hereditary) in place of representative" (149).

66. Stauffer, *The Humanness of John Calvin*, 47.

67. Ibid., 51, cited in Abel Lefranc, *La jeunesse de Calvin* (Paris, 1888), 70.

Whether he was in a university setting or drew on the experience of his teachers to assist him, Calvin was a more sociable man than is sometimes thought. He was a habitual letter writer, corresponding with jurists, governors, common people, and many ministers. These letters provide glimpses into the real Calvin. In these letters, he could refer to the affection he had for his teacher, Melchior Wolmar, and at the same time could mourn the passing of a ministerial friend as so staggering that it burdened him with grief.

The character and pulse of Calvinism impacted the world through a fraternity of devoted and committed friends. American theologian Douglas Kelly confirms that the Calvinistic tradition wielded influence far beyond Switzerland and France. Perhaps its most enduring legacy is its emphasis on the derived sovereignty of the people and the right to resist tyranny, a teaching that "would pass (indirectly and combined with ideas of very different parentage) into late seventeenth-century English political theories of human rights . . . [and] American debates on law and government."[68] No individual alone could sow so many seeds; these victories were scored by a team of colleagues.

Calvin was the premier but certainly not the only Protestant theorist. Other Reformers who were in his circle of friendship briskly articulated political works that were actually theologies of the state, with the following seminal works appearing in rapid succession in less than thirty years: Martin Bucer's *De Regno Christi* (1551), John Ponet's *A Short Treatise of Political Power* (1556), Christopher Goodman's *How Superior Powers ought to be obeyed of their subjects; and wherein they may lawfully by God's word be disobeyed and resisted* (1558), Peter Viret's *The World and the Empire* (1561), Francois Hotman's *Francogallia* (1573), Theodore Beza's *De Jure Magisterium* (1574), George Buchanan's *De Jure*

68. Douglas Kelly, *The Emergence of Liberty in the Modern World* (Phillipsburg, NJ: P&R Publishing, 1992), 37.

Regni Apud Scotos (1579), and Languet's *Vindiciae Contra Tyrannos* (1579). Each of these works legitimized the idea of citizen resistance against governmental expansion that exceeded proper limits. Interestingly, this bulk of political thought emanated from a tight circle of friends, most of whom were in contact with Calvin. It is hard to attribute such robust similarity of thought to accident.

Calvin's companionship with Theodore Beza is a model of friendship. Despite all the heady intellectual issues of the day and the challenges they brought, what most impressed Beza was Calvin's personal support and friendship. Thus Beza (and others) wrote about the camaraderie that Calvin shared with those around him. Calvin epitomized the modern notion of collegiality, and he was prudent enough to attract brilliant friends if at all possible. Once, when Beza was ill, Calvin admitted his own fear and deep sorrow upon learning of his colleague's illness. He wept and grieved, virtually staggering from the potential loss that might come to the church and to him personally. Fortunately, Beza recovered.

And there were many other friends besides Beza. The consensual strains of thought that flowed through the literary veins of Bullinger, Bucer, Viret, and Calvin—soon to be supplemented by Knox, Beza, Hotman, and Junius Brutus—formed an intellectual tradition with Geneva at its epicenter and Calvin as its father. His friendship with these scholars would prove to be the glue that held the movement together in its delicate infancy. J. H. Merle D'Aubigne noted this mutual interchange of ideas in these words:

> The catholicity of the Reformation is a noble feature in its character. The Germans pass into Switzerland; the French into Germany; in latter times men from England and Scotland pass over to the Continent, and doctors from the Continent into Great Britain. The reformers in the different countries spring up almost independently of one another, but no sooner are they

born than they hold out the hand of fellowship. . . . It has been an error, in our opinion, to write as hitherto, the history of the Reformation for a single country; the work is one.[69]

Calvin's associates served to stabilize and standardize an international movement.

Calvin, Farel, and Peter Viret were called "the tripod" or "three patriarchs," so well-known was their friendship. In Calvin's *Commentary on Titus*, he wrote that he did "not believe that there have ever been such friends who have lived together in such a deep friendship in their everyday style of life in this world as we have in our ministry."[70] Even when there were strong disagreements, Calvin was a paradigm of friendship. When these Reformers experienced family struggles or joys, Calvin shared those in his letters. These letters to various Reformers are full of sympathy and quick to illustrate a healthy loyalty. Moreover, his correspondence with refugees shows his great compassion. He even built bridges to Luther's disciples after the German leader denounced him. Calvin translated a theological work by Luther's chief disciple, Melanchthon.

What began in Geneva with a multi-national cadre of colleagues all seeking to extend the "republic of Christ" grew into a movement which featured theology, ideas, and a unique view of history that spread far beyond the city of Geneva alone.[71] With their confidence in God's providence and divine election, this circle of friends urged civil rulers to adopt their religious views and political practices "holding that no frontiers, no boundaries,

69. J. H. Merle D'Aubigne, *The History of the Reformation of the Sixteenth Century* (New York: American Tract Society, 1848), 3:416.

70. Stauffer, *The Humanness of John Calvin*, 57.

71. Duke, Lewis, and Pettegree, *Calvinism in Europe*, 200. This internationality, to some degree, blunts the suggestion by Hopfl that Geneva was unique in applying Calvinism because it was a relatively small political space in which the laws could be easily enforced. For his discussion, see Harro Hopfl, *The Christian Polity of John Calvin* (Cambridge: Cambridge University Press, 1982), 56–57.

no limits should confine the zeal of pious princes in the matter of God's glory and of the reign of Christ."[72] To some, their theology of resistance would appear politically subversive.

At times, as in any era, there were also disruptions of friendships. Calvin had to assist church members with broken relationships, and he had to deal with friction among the Protestant Reformers. No leader should expect that all will always go smoothly in the area of friendship; however, Calvin learned to encourage others around him, and he delegated certain responsibilities to his associates.

Richard Stauffer concluded that Calvin was far from "the isolated hero or the lonely genius that has often been pictured. Throughout his career, he had relationships with friends who show him unfailing affection and indefatigable devotion. If he exerted such charm, it is certainly because he himself had been such an incomparable friend. . . . For the devotion which one showed him, he paid the tribute of unswerving loyalty."[73] Following Calvin's death, it would become the task of his colleagues— exemplified by the statue of Beza in the famous sculpture on the Reformation Wall in Geneva—to spread the word.

Calvin's Death

The final five years of Calvin's life were gratifying, especially when contrasted with the valiant struggles in his early years. In the 1560s, he was permitted to watch the establishment and growth of the Academy, the astronomical rise in publishing, pastors being trained and sent into various locales, the stabilization of the city of Geneva, and the maturation of the church's presbytery. In addition, he began to be a sought-after advisor, and his work would outlast him.

72. Duke, Lewis, and Pettegre, *Calvinism in Europe*, 200.
73. Stauffer, *The Humanness of John Calvin*, 71.

The final years of his life were also characterized by chronic physical illness and an almost compulsive drive to write as much as possible. The final edition of the *Institutes* was completed in 1559, and most of Calvin's writings in his final five years were commentaries on biblical books and treatises on particular topics. As his life's curtain began to drop, the continuation of his work would be supported by the well-established reforms in Geneva and by wisely selected and carefully trained disciples. Calvin had succeeded as much as any other person to that point in history in finding ways to establish and multiply the ideas that fired his soul's passion.

Indeed, his own personal motto, "Here, Lord, I present my heart promptly and sincerely," with an icon of a heart aflame, was apt. His burning passion could not be extinguished, and his theology of action—once committed to writing—reached more people after his death than it did at the zenith of his popularity. His ideas were multiplied. On April 25, 1564, sensing the nearness of death, Calvin filed his final will. In it he pled his unworthiness ("Woe is me; my ardor and zeal have been so careless and languid, that I confess I have failed innumerable times"[74]) and thanked God for mercy. He appointed his brother, Anthony (whose reputation for divorcing an earlier wife due to adultery had been maliciously used to malign Calvin himself), to be his heir, and in his will he bequeathed equal amounts to the Boys' School, the poor refugees, and his stepdaughters. He also left part of his meager estate to his nephews and their children. To vindicate Calvin against charges of greed, Beza reiterated what Calvin had stated earlier: "If some will not be persuaded while I am alive, my death, at all events will show that I have not been a money-making man."[75] When his will was notarized and brought to the attention of the Senate,[76]

---

74. Beza, *Life of John Calvin*, 1:cxxv.
75. Ibid., 1:cxxxviii.
76. Beza refers to this Little Council as the "senate." See Ibid., 1:cxxii.

members of that council visited the declining Calvin to hear his final farewell personally.

Calvin's importance and relationship to the city leaders may be gleaned from his *Farewell Address to the Members of the Little Council.* [77] The members of this council had gone to his home to hear his advice and to express their appreciation for the "services he has performed for the Seigneurie and for that of which he has faithfully acquitted himself in his duty." A contemporary recorded Calvin's sentiments from April 27, 1564. In that chronicle, the dying Calvin first thanked these leaders for their support, cooperation, and friendship. Although they had engaged in numerous struggles, still their relationship was cordial. Even though he wished to accomplish more, Calvin humbly suggested that God might have "used him in the little he did." He urged the senators to honor God and to keep "hidden under the wings of God in whom all our confidence must be. And as much as we are hanging by a thread, nevertheless he will continue, as in the past, to keep us as we have already experienced that he saved us in several ways."

Calvin concluded by encouraging each one to "walk according to his station and use faithfully that which God gave him in order to uphold this Republic. Regarding civil or criminal trials, one should reject all favor, hate, errors, commendations." He also advised leaders not to aspire to privilege as if rank was a benefit for governors. "And if one is tempted to deviate from this," Calvin added, "one should resist and be constant, considering the One who established us, asking him to conduct us by his Holy Spirit, and he will not desert us."

Calvin's farewell to these political leaders was followed by his *Farewell Address to the Ministers* on April 28, 1564. From his chamber, Calvin reminded them poignantly:

77. This translation is from an unpublished translation of Calvin's "Farewell Address," trans. Kim McMahan of Oak Ridge, TN; originally published in 1999 at: http://capo.org/premise/99/jan/p990110.html.

> When I first came to this Church there was almost nothing.
> We preached and that was all. We searched out idols and
> burned them, but there was no reformation. Everything was
> in tumult. . . . I lived here through marvelous battles. I was
> welcomed with mockery one evening in front of my door by
> 50 or 60 rifle shots. Do you think that that could disturb
> a poor, timid student as I am, and as I have always been, I
> confess?[78]

The farewell address continued to review his Strasbourg exile,
the tensions he faced upon return, and some of his experiences
with various councils. Calvin concluded by predicting that the
battles would not lessen in the days ahead, warning, "You will be
busy after God takes me, even though I am nothing, still I know
I prevented three thousand uproars that there might have been
in Geneva. But take courage and strengthen yourselves, for God
will use this Church and will maintain her, and be sure that God
will keep her."

Calvin humbly confessed:

> I say again that all that I did has no value, and that I am a
> miserable creature. But if I could say what I truly wanted to,
> that my vices always displeased me, and that the root of the
> fear of God was in my heart, and you can say that what I was
> subjected to was good, and I pray that you would forgive me
> of the bad, but if there is anything good, that you conform
> yourselves to it and follow it.

He denied that he had written hateful things about others, and he confirmed that the pastors had elected Beza to be
his successor. "Watch that you help him [Beza]," exhorted the
dying Calvin, "for the duty is large and troublesome, of such
a sort that he may be overwhelmed under the burden. . . . As

78. Ibid.

for him, I know that he has a good will and will do what he can." Further, he requested that senators not change anything in Geneva's structures and urged them "not to innovate—we often ask for novelties—not that I desire for myself by ambition what mine remains, and that we retain it without wanting better, but because all change is hazardous, and sometimes harmful." The advice from this leader is filled with layer upon layer of wisdom.

Always sensitive to the calling to lead in many sectors of public life, he concluded with a plea for his fellow ministers to recall how they, too, would affect matters outside the walls of the church:

> Let each one consider the obligation he has, not only to this Church, but to the city, which has promised to serve in adversity as well as in prosperity, and likewise each one should continue in his vocation and not try to leave it or not practice it. For when one hides to escape the duty, he will say that he has neither thought about it nor sought this or that. But one should consider the obligation he has here before God.

When Calvin passed away almost a month after making these comments, on May 27, 1564, "the whole State regretted" the death of "its wisest citizen . . . a common parent." He was interred in a common cemetery at Plein Palais, finally finding the anonymity he craved. That, one historian wrote, was characteristic of Calvin in death as in life.[79] The widespread notice and sadness at his death should serve to correct any faulty view that Calvin's contemporaries either despised him or underestimated his importance. He was mourned, and his large number of friends would keep his memory alive far more than some contemporaries would have predicted.

79. Doumergue, *The Character of Calvin*, 173.

Epilogue

It may surprise some to conclude by citing humility as a chief virtue of Calvin's character. Some would not quickly identify that because Calvin has been so persistently (and wrongfully) vilified. However, a review of his life experiences illustrates Calvin's humility when:

- He acknowledged his admiration for Luther and other Reformers instead of viewing them as rivals to be criticized. He was not, in other words, the only leader on the block.
- He sought to serve out of the limelight instead of going on a lecture tour.
- He left Basle quietly after composing the *Institutes*, one of the classic pieces of Reformation literature.
- He humbly exited Geneva upon his first exile and did not hurl invectives at those who treated him so badly.
- He avoided seeking to be the only visible leader, often calling to his side those with equal or greater intellectual ability.
- He gladly served in the church and did not aspire to political or corporate power.
- When he was about to pass away, he evaluated his own accomplishments with considerable modesty.
- He did not design a system of corporate governance that gave him more authority than others.

Calvin understood the role of humility well. Indeed, he followed Augustine in viewing this as the prime virtue—almost the polar opposite of the prime vice, which was pride. One cannot help but see Calvin's emphasis on humility throughout his writings. After reviewing his life, perhaps this, as much as any other trait, helps us understand why his movement endured.

From the opening of the *Institutes*, Calvin noted that human beings could not know God or themselves apart from God's gracious revelation of himself to them in the Bible. It becomes very difficult to be proud if we confess that our very capacity to know is limited and dependent on God telling us how things work. Moreover, if we factor in the debilitating effects of the Adamic Fall, we also see how necessary it is both to turn to God as the fountain of any knowledge and also to admit our own intellectual inadequacy. To do so inspires humility.

On several occasions Calvin spoke clearly about the need for humility. In Book 3 of the *Institutes*, he urged his readers to lay aside private regard for themselves. Instead, they were called to divest themselves of "ambition and thirst for worldly glory."[80] The self-denial that he suggested diverts itself from vanity when one looks to God in all that he does.

As soon as this humble outlook seizes the mind, it leaves no room for "pride, show, or ostentation." Calvin urged leaders not to yearn for applause but instead to seek to reflect glory to God. He frequently criticized arrogance in its many forms. He was constantly on guard against self-flattery, which "sets up a kind of kingdom in his own breast." Arguing that we merely have what God gives, Calvin knew that there was no need to betray ingratitude by acting as though we have produced all goods ourselves. The knowledge that God is at work defines how much credit a human being can take. In fact, Calvin saw it as a rule of life that if "the hand of God is the ruler and arbiter of the fortunes of all," then "instead of rushing on with thoughtless violence" we accept "good and evil with perfect regularity."[81]

Calvin even explained that the elect, if they understood things correctly, would not take pride from their standing with God. In fact, the very idea that God does not save all people engenders humility.[82] Calvin contended: "If election precedes that divine grace by which we are made fit to obtain immortal life, what can God

80. *Institutes*, 3.7.2.
81. Ibid., 3.7.10.
82. Ibid., 3.21.1.

find in us to induce him to elect us?"[83] Calvin knew that divine sovereignty took away "all reference to worth;" moreover, he wrote, "It is just a clear declaration by the Lord that he finds nothing in men themselves to induce him to show kindness, that it is owing entirely to his own mercy, and, accordingly, that their salvation is his own work."[84] That, indeed, is humbling to one's pride!

The whole subject of human inability and limitations is only consistent with this emphasis on humility. While discussing the moral law, Calvin noted that natural law was definitely limited in how much information it would yield. Thus, the human mind was forced to turn to revealed law if it wished to find God's truths. Calvin emphasized the utter powerlessness of human ability and called on people to "distrust our own ability."[85]

In fact, Calvin's treatment of the law also called for humility. Since neither nature nor natural law yielded all the information needed to please God, Calvin noted that the very fact that God issued law signified that "we should learn true humility and self-abasement."[86] Man, in other words, may not be as proficient as he thinks he is in several areas. When one properly understands the law of God, that leads to reverence instead of pride, and when one sees how difficult this is to attain, the law humbles us by charging us both with impotence and unrighteousness.

The heart and soul of Calvin's theology requires and engenders humility if it is rightly understood. Arrogance, whether it pertains to human accomplishments or presumes that eternal election applies to a person who lives contrary to the ethical standards of God's election, is not a by-product of true Calvinism. It is true that distortions of Calvin's thought may yield such ideas, but a right understanding of how God works can only lead to human humility before the grand power of Almighty God. Followers of

83. Ibid., 3.22.2.
84. Ibid., 3.22.6.
85. Ibid., 2.8.3.
86. Ibid., 2.8.1.

Calvin's faith will better serve their people and organizations if they keep this balance prominent in their own lives.

Calvin's teachings and character seem to yield a particular kind of lifestyle and ethic by those who follow him. One who absorbs the character of Calvinism will exhibit a similar humility in the office, in the church, in the government, and in the home. Humility is characteristic of this great system of thought, and it was exemplified in the life of Calvin.

Nowhere was it more evident than in his comments about political leadership. Calvin's commentary on Daniel 6 illustrates many of the features of the life we are seeking to illuminate. Calvin displayed his suspicion of aggregate power in that commentary: "In the palaces of kings we often see men of brutal dispositions holding high rank, and we need not go back to history for this."[87] Of the low and contemptible character of some rulers, he wrote, "But now kings think of nothing else than preferring their own panders, buffoons, and flatterers; while they praise none but men of low character."[88] A prime example of the character expected of leaders is seen in this statement:

> It will always be deserving of condemnation when we find men selfishly pursuing their own advantage without any regard for the public good. Whoever aspires to power and self-advancement, without regarding the welfare of others must necessarily be avaricious and rapacious, cruel and perfidious. . . . The nobles of the realm [in Daniel's time] had no regard for the public good, but desired to seize upon all things for their own interests.[89]

Calvin sounded the alarm about leaders who were interested in power, comfort, or self-aggrandizement. Learned humility was

87. John Calvin, *Calvin's Commentaries* (Grand Rapids: Baker, 1979), 12:350.
88. Ibid.
89. Ibid.

an antidote for those vices; it was also a virtue for the leader who would leave such a legacy.

At the four hundredth anniversary of Calvin's death, J. I. Packer confirmed the effect of Calvin's humbling conversion in producing continuing humility both in his life and in his writings. Noted Packer:

> Conversion also made him *docile*. This, too, was a crucial ele-ment in Calvin's humility. We are thinking of Calvin as a ser-vant of God's Word—and a man must be divinely humbled before he becomes capable of this service. Proud man naturally leans to his own understanding; he would far rather speculate and follow his own ideas than listen to God speaking in Holy Scripture. Calvin, however, was humbled and made teachable by divine grace, and from then onward his overmastering intel-lectual concern was to learn the truth taught by Scripture; to function as a faithful echo of Scripture in his own teaching; and to make an accurate application of Scripture to men and situations. There never was a less speculative, less opinionated thinker than John Calvin. No theologian or preacher has ever been more consistently and exclusively dependent on Holy Scripture. Thus, though the *Institutio* is a work of tremendous power, learning, and ability, a book which reveals a truly stag-gering intellectual grasp at every point, one cannot read a page of it without realizing that, for all its positiveness of assertion and sharpness in controversy, it is fundamentally a humble book. Though learned, it is the very opposite of sophisticated; it reveals its author as a man of a simple, childlike spirit. For Calvin never says: this is my idea. He only ever says: this is what Scripture teaches. The author of the *Institutio* displays no other intellectual interest than to echo and explicate the written Word; in other words, to be a loyal servant of the Word of God.

Such, then, was John Calvin, the brilliant boy from Noyon, transformed by conversion into a God-centered, God-mastered, God-honoring man who bowed humbly to

God's will and listened humbly to God's Word, and whose tremendous powers of penetration and insight were put wholly at the service of Scripture. This was the man whom God could and did use to preserve Protestantism.[90]

John Calvin found that living his life in humility and service to the church and his community was his calling. Though that life was well-lived, it was not easily lived; yet, because he lived it the way he did, many of us, five centuries after his birth, are indebted to him and his service. His heart *was* sincerely and promptly offered.

90. J. I. Packer, "John Calvin: A Servant of the Word," in J. I. Packer, ed., *Puritan Papers*, vol. 3, *1963–1964* (Phillipsburg, NJ: P&R Publishing, 2001), 175–76.

Tributes: Measuring a Man
after Many Generations

Presbyterians often seek to claim Calvin as their own. Yet, others besides Presbyterians have found his life and thought to be worth emulating. Below are some tributes by Baptists, Anglicans, Independents, and Methodists. Of course, this is not an exhaustive catalogue—it is merely intended to illustrate that Calvin is esteemed by many evangelicals from differing traditions. Nor does it imply that those who admire Calvin do not part with him in some areas. The passage of time and the breadth of acclaim, however, is another measure of Calvin's contribution.

Baptists

Spurgeon

In the 1860s, Charles Haddon Spurgeon, the great London Baptist preacher had an opportunity to give his tribute to Calvin. One of Spurgeon's biographers, W. Y. Fullerton, recorded the following details.[1]

---

1. W. Y. Fullerton, *Charles Haddon Spurgeon: A Biography* (London: W. Williams and Norgate, 1920), available online at http://www.spurgeon.org/misc/bio6.htm.

The months of June and July, 1860 were given to a Continental tour; Mr. Spurgeon's first holiday in seven years. Belgium, the minor German states, and Switzerland were visited. The chief interest lies in his visit to Geneva, where he preached twice in Calvin's pulpit. "The first time I saw the medal of John Calvin, I kissed it," he says. "I preached in the Cathedral of St. Peter. I did not feel very comfortable when I came out in full canonicals, but the request was put to me in such a beautiful way that I could have worn the Pope's tiara if they had asked me. They said, 'Our dear brother comes to us from another country. Now when an ambassador comes from another country, he has a right to wear his own costume at court, but as a mark of a very great esteem, he sometimes condescends to the weakness of the country which he visits, and will wear court dress!' 'Well,' I said, 'yes, that I will, certainly; but I shall feel like running in a sack.' It was John Calvin's cloak, and that reconciled me to it very much."

Fullerton further noted that among the books Spurgeon valued most were Calvin's works. In the first volume of Calvin's commentaries in Spurgeon's library is written, "The volumes making up a complete set of Calvin were a gift to me from my own most dear and tender wife."

Fullerton said of Spurgeon that "nowhere does the whole personality stand out in such clear relief as in his sermons." The style of preaching used by both Calvin and Spurgeon was also very similar. Fullerton then provided the following estimate of Calvin, which he thought might have been written of Spurgeon with ever-so-slight alterations:

He was a born preacher. For years the spacious church of St. Pierre in Geneva was thronged, not once or twice, but several times a week to hear him. He was the star of the Genevan pulpit, but his words carried far beyond the city in which they were spoken. Seldom has any man addressed a wider audience or received a more grateful response. His sermons became models and standards for hundreds of pastors who were confined to such help as their publication supplied.

Admiral Coligny, warrior, diplomatist, and saint, was not the only one who made them his daily provender. It was on John Calvin's sermons on Ephesians that John Knox stayed his soul as he lay on his deathbed.

There is something of a perennially modern note in Calvin's preaching. He was not afraid to risk the charge of vulgarizing his theme by the use of the picturesque language of colloquial social intercourse. Whatever enabled him to grip the people's attention and penetrate to their consciences and hearts was legitimate. Much of his preaching was familiar talk poured forth by a man whose humanism could accord with a love for popular speech. If vernacular and classical alternatives presented themselves, the vernacular commonly received the preference.

Proverbs tripped from his tongue as though coined on the spot for the occasion, and gave agreeable piquancy to his words. Illustrations and metaphors he drew from all sources, sometimes surprising by their unexpectedness, coming from the lips of such a man. . . . Often he indulges in quite dramatic passages, making the characters with whom he is dealing express themselves in racy soliloquy or dialogue. Instead of making Moses, on receiving the order to ascend the mountain, point out how fatiguing and dangerous that would be for one of his years, Calvin pictures him as exclaiming, "That's all very fine! And I'm to go and break my legs climbing up there, am I? Of all things in the world! That's a fine prospect!"

Beza tells us that he despised ostentatious, pretentious eloquence. He held it wrong to seek to give brilliance and charm to God's Word by embellishment of language and subtleties of exposition. In his case the man was the style, and the man shaped the style. All was nervous, spirited, earnest, eager, mostly level to the intelligence of the humblest man who came to hear him, with that throb of suppressed passion often beating

through it which touches the fringes of one's consciousness as
the sound of a distant ... drum.

Fullerton, moreover, reviewed Spurgeon's conversion as an expression of Calvinism:

> These paragraphs, as we have said, might almost have been
> written of Spurgeon. And not only did he resemble the
> great Reformer in style, and in the number of sermons he
> preached—Calvin is supposed to have preached between
> three and four thousand—his heart was established in the
> same faith in God's sovereignty. "I can recall the day when I
> first received those truths into my soul," he says, and from
> his diary we know that day was April 7, 1850, "when they
> were, as John Bunyan says, burnt into my heart as with a
> hot iron; and I can recollect how I felt that I had grown on
> a sudden from a babe into a man, that I had found, once for
> all, the clue to the truth of God. One week-night, when I
> was sitting in the House of God—I was not thinking much
> about the preacher's sermon, for I did not believe it—the
> thought struck me, 'How did you come to be a Christian?' I
> sought the Lord. 'But how did you come to seek the Lord?'
> The truth flashed across my mind in a moment. I should
> not have sought Him unless there had been some previ-
> ous influence in my mind to make me seek Him. I prayed,
> thought I; but then I asked myself, 'How came I to pray?' I
> was induced to pray by reading the Scriptures. 'How came
> I to read the Scriptures?' Then in a moment I saw that God
> was at the bottom of it all, and that He was the Author of
> my faith; and so the whole doctrine of grace opened up to
> me, and from that doctrine I have not departed."
>
> "You may take a step from Paul to Augustine," Spurgeon
> once said to his students, "then from Augustine to Calvin,
> and then—well, you may keep your foot up a good while
> before you find such another." In another student talk he
> said that John Newton put Calvinism in his sermons as he

put sugar into his tea, his whole ministry was flavoured with it; then he added, "Don't be afraid of putting in an extra lump now and then."

Mr. Spurgeon was among the most eager celebrants of the tercentenary of Calvin's death on May 27, 1864. He agreed with John Knox, who said that in Geneva, in Calvin's day, was "the most perfect school of Christ that ever was on the earth since the days of the apostles."

Preaching in Leeds for the Baptist Union in a Methodist Chapel on a memorable occasion, he read the tenth chapter of Romans. Pausing at the thirteenth verse, he remarked, "Dear me! How wonderfully like John Wesley the apostle talked! '*Whosoever* shall call.' *Whosoever*. Why, that is a Methodist word, is it not?"

"Glory! Glory! Hallelujah!" came the responses.

"Yes, dear brothers," the preacher added, "but read the ninth chapter of the epistle, and see how wonderfully like John Calvin he talked— 'That the purpose of God according to election might stand.'" Smiles on the faces of those that had before been silent were the only response to this utterance.

In an 1855 sermon on election from 2 Thessalonians 2:13,14, Spurgeon spoke for himself:

It is no novelty, then, that I am preaching; no new doctrine. I love to proclaim these strong old doctrines, which are called by nickname Calvinism, but which are surely and verily the revealed truth of God as it is in Christ Jesus. By this truth I make a pilgrimage into the past, and as I go, I see father after father, confessor after confessor, martyr after martyr, standing up to shake hands with me. Were I a Pelagian, or a believer in the doctrine of free-will, I should have to walk for centuries all alone. Here and there a heretic of no very honorable character might rise up and call me brother. But taking these things to be the standard of my faith, I see the land of the ancients peopled with my brethren—I behold multitudes who confess the same as I do, and acknowledge that this is the religion of God's own church.

I also give you an extract from the old Baptist Confession. We are Baptists in this congregation—the greater part of us at any rate—and we like to see what our own forefathers wrote. Some two hundred years ago the Baptists assembled together, and published their articles of faith, to put an end to certain reports against their orthodoxy which had gone forth to the world. I turn to this old book . . . and I find the following as the 3rd Article: "By the decree of God, for the manifestation of his glory, some men and angels are predestinated, or foreordained to eternal life through Jesus Christ to the praise of his glorious grace; others being left to act in their sin to their just condemnation, to the praise of his glorious justice. These angels and men thus predestinated and foreordained, are particularly and unchangeably designed, and their number so certain and definite, that it cannot be either increased or diminished. Those of mankind that are predestinated to life, God, before the foundation of the world was laid, according to his eternal and immutable purpose, and the secret counsel and good pleasure of his will, hath chosen in Christ unto everlasting glory out of his mere free grace and love, without any other thing in the creature as condition or cause moving him "hereunto." As for these human authorities, I care not one rush for all three of them. I care not what they say, *pro* or *con*, as to this doctrine. I have only used them as a kind of confirmation to your faith, to show you that whilst I may be railed upon as a heretic and as a hyper-Calvinist, after all I am backed up by antiquity. All the past stands by me. I do not care for the present.

Give me the past and I will hope for the future. Let the present rise up in my teeth, I will not care. What though a host of the churches of London may have forsaken the great cardinal doctrines of God, it matters not. If a handful of us stand alone in an unflinching maintenance of the sovereignty of our God, if we are beset by enemies, ay, and even by our own brethren, who ought to be our friends and helpers, it matters not, if we can but count upon the past; the noble army of martyrs, the glorious host of confessors, are our friends; the witnesses of truth stand by us. With these for us, we will not say that we stand alone, but we may exclaim, "Lo, God hath reserved unto himself seven thousand that have not bowed the knee unto Baal." But the best of all is, God *is with us*. The great truth is always the Bible, and the Bible alone. My hearers, you do not believe in any other book than the Bible, do you? If I could prove this from all the books in Christendom; if I could fetch back the Alexandrian library, and prove it thence, you would not believe it any more; but you surely will believe what is in God's Word.

As the four hundredth anniversary of Calvin's death approached, D. M. Whyte summarized Spurgeon's Calvinism as follows.[2]

His boast was, "I am a true Calvinist after the order of John Calvin himself, and probably I have read more of his work than any of my accusers ever did." He admired Calvin because he believed that Calvin interpreted aright "the Old Gospel." He urges his students to read Calvin: "Of all commentators I believe John Calvin to be the most candid. In his expositions he is not always what moderns would call 'Calvinistic.' That is to say, where Scripture maintains the doctrine of Predestination and Grace he flinches in no degree, but inasmuch as some Scriptures bear the impress of human free action and responsibility, he does not shun to expound their meaning in all fairness and integrity."

Whyte also reports that for Spurgeon, Calvinism was shorthand for the essential gospel: "The doctrine which is called Calvinism

2. Quotes in this section are taken from D. M. Whyte, "Charles Haddon Spurgeon: Preacher," in J. I. Packer, ed., *Puritan Papers*, vol. 3, *1963–1964* (Phillipsburg, NJ: P&R Publishing, 2001), 78–79, 81.

did not spring from Calvinism. We believe that it sprang from the great Founder of all truth."

Professor Thomas Nettles of Southern Baptist Theological Seminary recently shared two other tributes from nineteenth-century Southern Baptist leaders.

John Broadus, who dominated homiletics classrooms for decades, shared the conviction of *James P. Boyce* that, among the historic options concerning the systematic exhibition of biblical doctrine, Calvinism most nearly approximated an accurate and clearly expressed understanding of biblical truth. Broadus believed that it "compels an earnest student to profound thinking, and . . . makes him at home among the most inspiring and ennobling views of God and of the universe he has made." Broadus recalled a deeply pious layman in First Baptist Church, Richmond, whose "profound thinking upon the greatest themes of theology often surprised his ministerial friends." Broadus immediately continued his observations, "Calvinism compels to deep thinking. One must not dare to say that this makes any person dislike Calvinism, but it certainly attracts some minds toward it."[3]

Not only did Calvinism provoke serious theological reflection, but Broadus also believed it to be the purest form of biblical theology. In his recollection of the influence of Charles Hodge of Princeton on the thinking of Basil Manly Jr. and James P. Boyce, Broadus pointed in particular to "that exalted system of Pauline truth which is technically called Calvinism." In lectures delivered at Newton Theological Institution in May, 1876, Broadus called Augustine "the father of the theology of the Protestant Reformation." Luther highly valued Augustine, virtually next to the Bible, and Calvin "reduced Augustine's doctrines to a religious form." Little is lost, however, in the transition from Paul to Calvin for "What we call

3. John A. Broadus, *In Memorial of James Thomas, Jr.* (Richmond, 1888), 52.

Calvinism is the doctrine of Paul, developed by Augustine and systematized by Calvin."[4]

Broadus's views on this changed little if any during his life of rigorous scholarship. In September, 1891, on a trip to Europe given him by his students, Broadus went to Geneva by steamer on the Rhine. One of the five governors of Geneva was named Turretin. This fact certainly would interest the Latin theology students at the seminary. After a lofty commendation of Francis Turretin's noble work on systematic theology, Broadus observed,

> The people who sneer at what is called Calvinism might as well sneer at Mont Blanc. We are not in the least bound to defend all of Calvin's opinions or actions, but I do not see how any one who really understands the Greek of the Apostle Paul or the Latin of Calvin and Turretin can fail to see that these latter did but interpret and formulate substantially what the former teaches.[5]

Ernest Reisinger also gathers testimony for Calvin's view of election from many American Baptist sources. He introduces the following witnesses, wishing to show "that it is not only in the Bible, but our Baptist fathers believed it, taught it and preached it."[6]

> JOHN A. BROADUS, former president of the Southern Baptist Theological Seminary: *"From the divine side, we see that the Scriptures teach an eternal election of men to eternal life simply out of God's good pleasure."*

4. John A. Broadus, *Lectures on the History of Preaching* (A. C. Armstrong and Son, 1902), 81.

5. A. T. Robertson, *Life and Letters of John A. Broadus* (Harrisonburg, VA: Sprinkle, 2004), 396–97.

6. Ernest Reisinger, "A Southern Baptist Looks at the Biblical Doctrine of Election," available online at: http://www.founders.org/library/reis1/reis.html.

B. H. CARROLL, founder and first president of the Southwestern Baptist Seminary: *"Every one that God chose in Christ is drawn by the Spirit to Christ. Every one predestined is called by the Spirit in time, and justified in time, and will be glorified when the Lord comes."*

JAMES P. BOYCE, founder and first president of Southern Baptist Seminary: *"God, of His own purpose, has from eternity determined to save a definite number of mankind as individuals, not for or because of any merit or works of theirs, nor of any value of them to Him; but of His own good pleasure."*

W. T. CONNER, professor of theology, Southwestern Baptist Seminary, Fort Worth, Texas: *"The doctrine of election means that God saves in pursuance of an eternal purpose. This includes all the gospel influence, work of the Spirit and so on, that leads a man to repent of his sins and accept Christ. So far as man's freedom is concerned, the doctrine of election does not mean that God decrees to save a man irrespective of his will. It rather means that God purposes to lead a man in such a way that he will freely accept the gospel and be saved."*

CHARLES HADDON SPURGEON, The Prince of Preachers, in a sermon delivered on Matthew 24:24 (April 22, 1860): *"I do not hesitate to say, that next to the doctrine of the crucifixion and the resurrection of our blessed Lord—no doctrine had such prominence in the early Christian church as the doctrine of the election of Grace."*

If Spurgeon is correct (and he is) there sure have been a lot of preachers successful in avoiding a very important and prominent Bible truth. Spurgeon said, "There seems to be an inveterate prejudice in the human mind against this doctrine, and although most other doctrines will be received by professing Christians, some with caution, others with pleasure, yet this one seems to be most frequently disregarded and discarded."

If it were true in Spurgeon's day, I wonder what he would say now when most pulpits are silent about it, and therefore, the pews ignorant of it.

The Old Baptist Confessions, such as, The Baptist Confession of 1689 (London Confession); The Philadelphia Confession of 1742; The New Hampshire Confession—all these confessions are crystal clear on the blessed doctrine of Sovereign Election.

There is no doctrine so grossly neglected and misrepresented in all the Bible. One of our Fathers said, *"From hostile lips a fair and correct statement of the doctrine of election is never heard."*

The treatment the doctrine of election receives from the hands of its enemies is much like that received by the early Christians from pagan Roman Emperors. The early Christians were often clothed in the skins of animals and then subjected to attack by ferocious wild beasts. So the doctrine of election is often clothed in ugly garb and held up to ridicule and erroneous attacks.

John Piper

Closer to our own time, well-known Baptist pastor John Piper gave an address to the 1997 Bethlehem Conference for Pastors entitled "The Divine Majesty of the Word: John Calvin: The Man and His Preaching." Pertinent excerpts below show Piper's esteem for Calvin.[7]

Beginning with an affirmation of the sovereignty and self-existence of God from Exodus 3:14, Piper called his fellow evangelicals to recognize that Calvin's respect and passion for the majesty of God led him to confront the Roman Catholicism

---

7. The sermon is available online at http://www.desiringgod.org/Resource Library/Biographies/1471_The_Divine_Majesty_of_the_Word/.

of his day, along with its leaders (such as Cardinal Sadolet). Piper notes:

> Calvin's response to Sadolet is important because it uncovers the root of Calvin's quarrel with Rome that will determine his whole life—as well as the shape of this lecture. The issue is not, first, justification or priestly abuses or transubstantiation or prayers to saints or papal authority. All those will come in for discussion. But beneath all of them, the fundamental issue for John Calvin, from the beginning to the end of his life, was the issue of the centrality and supremacy and majesty of the glory of God. He sees in Sadolet's letter the same thing Newbigin sees in self-centered Evangelicalism.

Piper viewed Calvin as rebuking Sadolet for not holding the name of God in highest sanctity: "And this was Calvin's chief contention with Rome. It comes out in his writings over and over again. He goes on and says to Sadolet that what he should do—and what Calvin aims to do with all his life—is 'set before [man], as the prime motive of his existence, *zeal to illustrate the glory of God.*'" Piper continues:

> I think this would be a fitting banner over all of John Calvin's life and work—*zeal to illustrate the glory of God.* The essential meaning of John Calvin's life and preaching is that he recovered and embodied a passion for the absolute reality and majesty of God. That is what I want you to see. Benjamin Warfield said of Calvin, "No man ever had a profounder sense of God than he." There's the key to Calvin's life and theology. . . . It's this relentless orientation on the glory of God that gives coherence to John Calvin's life and to the Reformed tradition that followed. Vos said that the "all-embracing slogan of the Reformed faith is this: the work of grace in the sinner as a *mirror for the glory of God.*" Mirroring the glory of God is the meaning of John Calvin's life and ministry.

For Calvin, the need for the Reformation was fundamentally this: Rome had "destroyed the glory of Christ in many ways—by calling upon the saints to intercede, when Jesus Christ is the one mediator between God and man; by adoring the Blessed Virgin, when Christ alone shall be adored; by offering a continual sacrifice in the Mass, when the sacrifice of Christ upon the Cross is complete and sufficient," by elevating tradition to the level of Scripture and even making the word of Christ dependent for its authority on the word of man. Calvin asks, in his *Commentary on Colossians*, "How comes it that we are 'carried about with so many strange doctrines' (Hebrews 13:9)?" And he answers, "Because the excellence of Christ is not perceived by us." In other words, the great guardian of Biblical orthodoxy throughout the centuries is a passion for the glory and the excellency of God in Christ. Where the center shifts from God, everything begins to shift everywhere. Which does not bode well for doctrinal faithfulness in our own non-God-centered day.

Piper summarizes:

Therefore, the unifying root of all of Calvin's labors is his passion to display the glory of God in Christ. When he was 30 years old, he described an imaginary scene of himself at the end of his life, giving an account to God, and said, "The thing [O God] at which I chiefly aimed, and for which I most diligently labored, was, that the glory of thy goodness and justice . . . might shine forth conspicuous, that the virtue and blessings of thy Christ . . . might be fully displayed." Twenty-four years later, unchanged in his passions and goals, and one month before he actually did give an account to Christ in heaven (he died at age 54), he said in his last will and testament, "I have written nothing out of hatred to anyone, but I have always faithfully propounded what I esteemed to be *for the glory of God.*"

Piper notes Calvin's "self-conscious choice" upon his return to Geneva in September 1541 after his exile in Strasbourg to resume preaching right where he left off on Easter 1538. Piper sees in that a "remarkable commitment to the centrality of sequential expository preaching." For Calvin, there are three valid reasons for the kind of preaching that elevates the text, then and now.

First, Calvin believed that the Word of God was a lamp that had been taken away from the churches. He said in his own personal testimony, "Thy word, which ought to have shone on all thy people like a lamp, was taken away, or at least suppressed as to us. . . . And now, O Lord, what remains to a wretch like me, but . . . earnestly to supplicate thee not to judge according to [my] deserts that fearful abandonment of thy word from which, in thy wondrous goodness thou hast at last delivered me." Calvin reckoned that the continuous exposition of books of the Bible was the best way to overcome the "fearful abandonment of [God's] Word."

Second, Parker says that Calvin had a horror of those who preached their own ideas in the pulpit. He said, "When we enter the pulpit, it is not so that we may bring our own dreams and fancies with us." He believed that by expounding Scripture as a whole, he would be forced to deal with all that *God* wanted to say, not just what *he* might want to say.

Third—and this brings us full circle to the beginning, where Calvin saw the majesty of God in his word—he believed with all his heart that the Word of God was indeed the Word of *God*, and that all of it was inspired and profitable and radiant with the light of the glory of God. In Sermon number 61 on Deuteronomy he challenged us: Let the pastors boldly dare all things *by the word of God. . . .* Let them constrain all the power, glory, and excellence of the world to give place to and to obey *the divine majesty of this word.* Let them enjoin everyone by it, from the highest to the lowest. Let them edify the body of Christ. Let them devastate Satan's reign. Let them pasture the sheep, kill the wolves, instruct and exhort the rebellious. Let them bind and loose thunder and lightning, if necessary, *but let them do all according to the word of God."*

The key phrase here is "the divine majesty of this word." This was always the root issue for Calvin. How might he best show forth for all of Geneva and all of Europe and all of history the divine majesty? He answered with a life of continuous expository preaching. There would be no better way to manifest the full range of the glories of God and the majesty of his being than to spread out the full range of God's Word in the context of the pastoral ministry of shepherding care.

My own conviction is that this is why preaching remains a central event in the life of the church even 500 years after the printing press and the arrival of radio and TV and cassettes and CD's and computers. God's word is mainly about the majesty of God and the glory of God. That is the main issue in ministry. And, even though the glory and majesty of God in his word can be known in the still small voice of whispered counsel by the bedside of a dying saint, there is something in it that cries out for expository exultation. This is why preaching will never die. And radical, pervasive God-centeredness will always create a hunger for preaching in God's people. If God is "I am who I am"—the great, absolute, sovereign, mysterious, all-glorious God of majesty whom Calvin saw in Scripture, there will always be preaching, because the more this God is known and the more this God is central, the more we will feel that he must not just be analyzed and explained, he must be acclaimed and heralded and magnified with expository exultation.

Steven Lawson

Steven Lawson's recent work, *The Expository Genius of John Calvin*, gives another full tribute to how helpful Calvin is for preaching. Moreover, the Founders movement (see www. founders.org) within the Southern Baptist Convention has frequent tributes to the virtues of Calvinism.

Anglicans

J. I. Packer

From Baptists of a low-church persuasion to those of a higher liturgical tradition, the voice of James I. Packer has clearly trumpeted Calvinism for over fifty years.[8] Packer puts it succinctly at one point:

> The internal witness of the Spirit in John Calvin is a work of enlightenment whereby, through the medium of verbal testimony, the blind eyes of the spirit are opened, and divine realities come to be recognized and embraced for what they are. This recognition Calvin says, is as immediate and unanalysable as the perceiving of a color, or a taste, by physical sense—an event about which no more can be said than that when appropriate stimuli were present it happened, and when it happened we know it had happened.

Elsewhere, Packer is equally clear when he speaks of the abiding value of Calvinism. At the four hundredth anniversary of Calvin's death, for example, Packer summarized his appreciation of Calvinism in the following terms.[9]

> It is now four hundred years since John Calvin died. Why should we concern ourselves with him today? Why should we regard him as a man worthy of commemoration at the present time?
>
> It would be answer enough to this question simply to point out that his influence on history was so immense that you cannot begin to explain modern Britain—England, Wales, Scot-

---

8. For more, see J. I. Packer, "Calvin the Theologian," in *John Calvin: A Collection of Essays* (Grand Rapids: Wm. B. Eerdmans Publishing Co., 1966).

9. J. I. Packer, "John Calvin: A Servant of the Word," in J. I. Packer, ed., *Puritan Papers, Volume 3: 1963–1964* (Phillipsburg, NJ: P&R Publishing, 2001), 165–67, 191–92.

land, and Ireland—nor modern Europe, nor modern America, nor indeed any English-speaking country anywhere, without making reference to him. You cannot leave him out of the story of any part of the Western world.

It is not always realized, but it is true none the less, that for a century and more after his death John Calvin was quite literally the world's most influential man, in the sense that his ideas made more history than did the thoughts, or actions, of anyone else who was alive at the time. The epoch from the middle of the sixteenth century to the beginning of the age of Newton, in the last quarter of the century following, was in truth the age of Calvin.

Packer continues to ascribe affectionately:

Without Calvin, Protestantism might well not have survived beyond the middle of the seventeenth century; for it is a matter of simple fact that the only Protestants who were prepared to stand and fight, to the last ditch if necessary, against Roman and Erastian tyranny, were the Calvinists. If we look at more recent history, and think of men like Edwards, Brainerd, Whitefield, Howell Harris, Wilberforce, Spurgeon, Carey, Henry Martyn, Moffat, Paton, and McCheyne, we see at once that the evangelical movement which began with revival in the eighteenth century, and the social and missionary movements which overflowed from it throughout the nineteenth century, could not have been what they were without John Calvin; for these great leaders, and a host of others who stood with them, were all Calvinists in their basic creed.

Thus we may fairly say that if we are going to understand our religious and cultural heritage in this mid-twentieth century, it is absolutely essential that we should know something about Calvin. And that in itself would be sufficient reason for commemorating him now.

But my main reason for asking you to join me at this time in thankful recollection of John Calvin is that he is in a real sense a prophet for today, a man with a message for us and for our times. In his own life, he was God's man for a crisis, ministering to a Europe that was in turmoil. And, though comparisons between one age and another are notoriously risky, and can easily mislead those who make them, I think it is quite certainly true that, so far as basic attitudes are concerned, no age since has been more like Calvin's than our own. At a deep level, our times are like his, and his teaching speaks directly to our own present need. An American tribute to Calvin, published in 1959, was entitled *John Calvin: Contemporary Prophet*. This estimate of Calvin's significance for us is, in my judgment, sober truth.

Packer then elaborates several cultural and doctrinal similarities that yoked over four centuries of Calvinism. In terms of cultural similarity between 1564 and 1964, he cited: (1) global political unrest; (2) the denigration of Christian civilization; and (3) a widespread religious confusion and ignorance. Furthermore, this religious confusion focused, for Packer, on three great theological issues: (1) biblical authority; (2) grace and salvation; and (3) church unity.

Packer concludes his insightful tribute with this summary:

> At the heart of Calvin's Christianity there was a vision and a passion. The vision was of God on the throne, God reigning in majesty. How often Calvin used the words "majesty" and "glory"! How often he dilates on the greatness of God! The passion corresponded to the vision. It was the passion expressed in that great phrase which has become the slogan of Calvinism—*soli Deo gloria*! It was the longing that the Almighty Creator and Redeemer, the Source and Stay and End of all things, should receive the praise and worship and adoration that were His due.
>
> Warfield insists that this passion, with the vision from which it derives, is the formative principle of Calvinism. He stresses that the focal center of the Calvinistic outlook

is not justification, or predestination, or the "five points," crucial though all these things are, but something greater still—not just a view of salvation, but first and foremost a view of God. What view of God? Well, Warfield puts it in better words than I can muster, so let me simply quote to you what he says,

> It is the vision of God and His Majesty ... which lies at the foundation of the entirety of Calvinistic thinking. ... The Calvinist is the man who has seen God, and who, having seen God in His glory, is filled on the one hand, with a sense of his own unworthiness to stand in God's sight as a creature, and much more as a sinner, and on the other hand, with adoring wonder that nevertheless this God is a God who receives sinners. He who believes in God without reserves and is determined that God shall be God to him, in all his thinking, feeling, willing—in the entire compass of his life activities, intellectual, moral, spiritual—throughout all his individual, social, religious relations—is ... by the very necessity of the case, a Calvinist.

And if Calvin could come back, he would tell us, I think, that our God was too small; and he would ask us whether we had ever seen the vision of God on His throne; and he would ask us to let him show it to us. "In your world that is shaken to its foundations by political and cultural convulsions, in days when your churches are weak and starving, in a time of fear and depression and discouragement," Calvin would say to us, "this is the vision you need; and it is a vision that God will give you from His Word, as He gave it to me; all that you need is to learn to listen to what He says." And then perhaps Calvin would point us to such a passage as Psalm 93, where the whole Calvinistic vision, and with it the whole Calvinistic confidence and the whole Calvinistic passion, is summed up.[10]

10. Ibid., 192.

Packer, among modern Anglicans, knows the heart of Calvinism. And that understanding leads others, who correctly spy the genius of Calvinism as rooted in the majesty of God, to agree with Calvin that our hearts should be sincerely and promptly offered to the Lord.

J. C. Ryle

Slightly earlier than Packer, another well-known Anglican Calvinist saw the value of Calvin in many areas. In a tract on election, J. C. Ryle, a late nineteenth-century Anglican Bishop of Liverpool stated:

> Some tell us that at any rate Election is not the doctrine of the Church of England. It may do very well for dissenters and presbyterians, but not for churchmen. 'It is a mere piece of Calvinism,' they say,—'an extravagant notion which came from Geneva, and deserves no credit among those who love the Prayer-book.' Such people would do well to look at the end of their Prayer-books, and to read the Thirty-nine Articles. Let them turn to the 17th Article, and mark the following words . . . I commend that Article to the special attention of all English Churchmen. It is one of the sheet-anchors of sound doctrine in the present day. It never can be reconciled with baptismal regeneration! A wiser statement of the true doctrine of personal Election was never penned by the hand of uninspired man. It is thoroughly well-balanced and judiciously proportioned. In the face of such an Article it is simply ridiculous to say that the Church of England does not hold the doctrine of this paper.[11]

In another tract, Ryle, while extolling the piety and theology of the English hymn writer Augustus Toplady, said,

> On all these subjects I hold firmly that Calvin's theology is much more scriptural than the theology of Arminius. In a

11. The tract is available online at http://www.tracts.ukgo.com/ryle_election.doc.

word, I believe that Calvinistic divinity is the divinity of the
Bible, of Augustine, and of the Thirty-nine Articles of my own
Church, and of the Scotch Confession of Faith.... Well would
it be for the Churches, if we had a good deal more of clear,
distinct, sharply-cut doctrine in the present day! Vagueness
and indistinctness are marks of our degenerate condition.[12]

Ryle went further, though. While he did not agree with the
way Toplady verbally attacked his enemies, he did not shy away
from admiring the "extraordinary ability" of many of his polemical
writings. "For example," Ryle wrote,

[Toplady's] 'Historic Proof of the Doctrinal Calvinism of
the Church of England' is a treatise that displays a prodi-
gious amount of research and reading. It is a book that no
one could have written who had not studied much, thought
much, and thoroughly investigated an enormous mass of
then logical literature. You see at once that the author has
completely digested what he has read, and is able to concentrate all his reading on every point which he handles.
The best proof of the book's ability is the simple fact that
down to the present day it has never been really answered.
It has been reviled, sneered at, abused, and held up to scorn.
But abuse is not argument. The book remains to this hour
unanswered, and that for the simplest of all reasons, that
it is unanswerable. It proves irrefragably, whether men like
it or not, that Calvinism is the doctrine of the Church of
England, and that all her leading divines, until Laud's time,
were Calvinists.

For more of Ryle's admiration of the debt owed to the Protestant
Reformation, see his "What Do We Owe to the Reformation?"[13] In

12. Available online at http://www.tracts.ukgo.com/ryle_toplady.doc.
13. Available online at http://www.tracts.ukgo.com/ryle_owe_reform
ation.doc.

that essay he concluded: "My own mind is fully made up. I say the Church of England had better perish and go to pieces than forsake the principles of the Reformation, and tolerate the Sacrifice of the Mass and Auricular Confession. But whether she is to perish or not depends, under God, on the action of her members."

Independents

John MacArthur

Contemporary American evangelical John MacArthur is one of the finest living expositors in Calvin's tradition. In his "Insights into a Pastor's Heart," MacArthur says: "we then give our whole lives to the Word of God. We go deep into it and we lift our people high in praise."[14] MacArthur then refers to B. B. Warfield's estimate that no one had a more profound sense of God's glory than John Calvin. "And that was the key to his theology and the key to his influence."

In a slightly fuller version of this thought, MacArthur noted at length:

> Lesslie Newbigin in a CT [*Christianity Today*] article in '96 says, "I suddenly saw that someone could use all the language of evangelical Christianity and yet the center was fundamentally the self and God was auxiliary to that." Now that defines the contemporary church and contemporary preaching, it's all about you and your comfort, it's all about you and your soul, it's all about you and fixing you, and helping you, and bumping you up a few notches on the comfort scale. And it's a far cry from where Martin Luther was. It's a far cry from where John Calvin was. I've been reading a lot about John Calvin lately because I've been in Geneva a couple of times and was able with John Glass to

14. John MacArthur, "Insights into a Pastor's Heart," available online at http://www.gty.org/resources/transcripts/GTY71.

dig a little more deeply into some of the things in Geneva that reveal the nature of the man, the character of the man. B. B. Warfield said this about Calvin and probably this is as defining as anything that's been said about John Calvin. B. B. Warfield said about Calvin, "No man ever had a profounder sense of God than he. . . ."

When you go back and you ask yourself . . . where do I find the deepest understanding of theology? You see it coming out of the reformed faith, don't you? Where do I go back and find the highest expressions of prayer? You find it in the same place, don't you because it is the depth that creates the height.

The reason Calvin had such an incredible sense of God, a profound sense of God was that his entire ministry was exposition. Many people think John Calvin, they think of *The Institutes* which were written by his early twenties and refined five times through his life, but what many people don't know is he was a Bible expositor.[15]

In one address, MacArthur even speaks of his recent visit to Geneva and provides a short life of Calvin. Elsewhere MacArthur commends Calvin's view of assurance as being at the heart of faith and frequently quotes Calvin's work approvingly, particularly his comments on John 17. MacArthur also agrees with Calvin on the errors of Roman Catholicism, the days of creation, prayer, the depravity of man, and fasting. (Of course, MacArthur disagrees with Calvin on matters like the sacraments, church government, and the end times.)

In one Reformation Sunday sermon, MacArthur even referred with pride to his two-year old grandson: Calvin. He also informed his congregation that he had

a copy of the 1599 Geneva Bible with the Book of Common Prayer in front and the Psalter in the back, the hymn book, so they had every thing in one volume. . . . The Geneva

15. Ibid.

Bible that came out of Geneva under the leadership of Calvin and Knox and some others was translated into those various languages. It's really that that has given us our heritage of the Christian faith so it is something to think back and to remember as an absolutely critical milestone in the work of the spirit and the world.[16]

Methodists

In his 1964 essay on Calvin,[17] Martyn Lloyd-Jones also tied Calvin to the eighteenth-century British Methodist evangelist, George Whitefield. Lloyd-Jones began his essay commemorating the four-hundredth anniversary of Calvin's death by noting several strong similarities between Calvin and Whitefield. Both, he said, were "Paulinists," and both were "men who longed, perhaps more than any of their contemporaries, for unity among evangelicals." Commented Lloyd-Jones on the occasion:

Calvin was tremendously concerned that all Reformed and Evangelical people should come together in unity. He bemoaned the divisions and the differences that had arisen, and he was prepared to do anything he could—he said he was ready to cross, if necessary, ten seas in order to attend a conference which would help to promote this unity among Reformed Evangelical people.

Dr. Lloyd-Jones also admired the preaching ability of Whitefield and Calvin: "How one man was able to do it all, and to preach so regularly in addition, is very amazing for us to contemplate. Exactly the same thing is true of Whitefield." Some of Lloyd-Jones' highest praise, though, is reserved for Calvin as an exemplar of

16. John MacArthur, "Marks of a Faithful Church," available online at http://www.gty.org/Resources/Print/transcripts/2751.

17. D. Martyn Lloyd-Jones, "John Calvin and George Whitefield," in J. I. Packer, ed., *Puritan Papers*, 3:223–24.

humility: "The teaching of John Calvin humbles man in the first instance; it glorifies God. It makes man feel that he is insignificant, that he is nobody; and however much a man may be privileged or enabled to do, he knows that it is God Who does it. That is the other thing in which he is interested. Of course, Calvin would have grown red-faced to hear such praise."

Even clearer, Lloyd-Jones gave a synopsis of Calvin's value in a BBC address on June 25, 1944. Amidst the shrapnel of World War II, one of the strongest preachers in London took the opportunity to extol Calvin.[18] In the mid-twentieth century, Lloyd-Jones thought it remarkable that over the preceding twenty years, Calvin had been making somewhat of a comeback. He noted that, prior to this period, little respect was given to Calvin, and if one admired Calvin, that admirer was thought of "as a cruel, masterly, hard person." Calvin was routinely characterized as oppressive, and he was viewed as smithing the leg-irons of dour Puritanism. Calvin's influence was pejoratively viewed as a monstrosity in a dank museum of theology.

For several reasons (and Karl Barth is given some credit for this), Calvinist groups began to crop up all over the world at this time, and the International Calvinistic Congress met in Edinburgh in 1938. American conferences were held as well. Lloyd-Jones then provides a brief biographical sketch of Calvin before returning to comment on the Reformer's abiding value. Of his "summa theologica of Protestantism and the clearest declaration which the evangelical faith has ever had"—high praise, to be sure—Lloyd-Jones said:

> Luther was a volcano, spewing out fiery ideas in all directions
> without much pattern or system. But ideas cannot live and last

18. D. Martyn Lloyd-Jones, "John Calvin," in his *Knowing the Times: Addresses Delivered on Various Occasions, 1942–1977* (Edinburgh: The Banner of Truth Trust, 1989), 32–37. One of my friends, B. B. Negron, brought this work to my attention, and I am indebted to him.

without a body, and the great need of the Protestant movement in the last days of Luther was for a theologian with the ability to arrange and to express the new faith within a system. That person was Calvin. . . . It was he who saved Protestantism by giving it a body of theology within his *Institutes*; and it is from this that the faith and theology of most of the Protestant churches have sprung. . . . On the *Institutes* was based the faith of the Puritans, and the history of Switzerland and Holland cannot be explained except in this context.

Lloyd-Jones spied Calvin's "main feature" as being thoroughly based on the Bible, not resorting to a mixture of secular sources or even the earlier church fathers. "It is," remarked Lloyd-Jones, "in the *Institutes* that one gets biblical theology for the first time, rather than dogmatic theology." For Calvin, revelation was not a supplement to reason, and for him "the great central and all-important truth was the sovereignty of God and God's glory. We must start here and everything else issues from here."

Lloyd-Jones concluded this brief radio address by urging Christians to understand that

this is God's world, that every gift which man possesses is a gift from God, that men are all one as sinners before God, and that no king, nor any other, has a right to tyrannize his fellow men. We must have order, we must have discipline. Man has a right to freedom, but not to free license. That is the essence of Calvin's teaching. He worked it out minutely to cover every aspect of life.

Indeed, that comprehensiveness is one of the explanations for Calvinism's enduring vitality.

Five years later, when an edition of the *Institutes* was republished by James Clarke (1949), Lloyd-Jones spoke of it as "the best news I have heard for some time." On the cover blurb for that work, he further described this classic as "most moving, and at times thrilling" and "deeply devotional." The erstwhile Welsh Methodist opined that this republication was also a tome for the times:

> In a world which is shaking in its very foundations and which lacks any ultimate authority, nothing is so calculated to strengthen and to stabilize one's soul as this magnificent exposition and outworking of the glorious doctrine of the sovereignty of God. It was the 'iron ration of the soul' of the Reformation martyrs, of the Pilgrim Fathers, the Covenanters, and many others who have had to face persecution and death for Christ's sake.

John Wesley

John Wesley himself, though definitely not a follower of Calvin, at least described his work honestly and expressed some appreciation. In his article, "Predestination Calmly Considered," Wesley referred to the Westminster Confession of Faith and showed that he understood Calvin's thought well.[19] In Wesley's 1765 "Of Asperio Vindicated," he ascribed, "I believe Calvin was a great instrument of God; and that he was a wise and pious man; But I cannot but advise those who love his memory to let Servetus alone. Yet if any one resolves to understand the whole affair," he may consult a learned account by a Dr. Chandler of London.[20]

Later in his "What Is an Arminian?" Wesley argued against using either "Arminian" or "Calvinist" as essentially pejorative terms. After describing the thought of Jacob Arminius and

19. John Wesley, "Predestination Calmly Considered," in *The Works of John Wesley* (1872; repr. Grand Rapids: Zondervan), 10:204–5. For these references to Wesley, I wish to thank my friend, the Rev. W. Laurens Hudson, Southern District Superintendent for the Evangelical Methodist Church.

20. Wesley, "Of Asperio Vindicated," in *The Works of John Wesley*, 10:351.

identifying accurately several key differences between Calvin and Arminus, Wesley acknowledged and charged:

> Let no man bawl against Arminians, till he knows what the term means; and then he will know that Arminians and Calvinists are just upon a level. And Arminians have as much right to be angry at Calvinists, as Calvinists have to be angry at Arminians. John Calvin was a pious, learned, sensible man; and so was James Harmens [Arminius]. Many Calvinists are pious, learned, sensible men; and so are many Arminians. Only the former hold absolute predestination; the latter, conditional.[21]

A well-known German Lutheran, Valentine Andreae, visiting Geneva after Beza's death and a half-century after Calvin's, praised the city for "the perfect institut[ion] of a perfect republic." Armed with moral accountability, the Genevans had virtually eliminated the vices so characteristic of other places. Andreae claimed that, if not for his commitment to Lutheran tradition, he "would have forever been chained to that place by the agreement in morals, and I have ever since tried to introduce something like it into our churches."[22]

Roman Catholic

And finally a voice from the Roman Catholic tradition may be added. Alexandre Ganoczy estimated that Calvin was "superior to Luther in his careful biblical and patristic documentation," noting:

> As a young theologian, Calvin cannot be compared to a musical performer or to an orchestra conductor whose task is limited

21. Wesley, "What Is an Arminian?" in *The Works of John Wesley*, 10:360.
22. Cited in Philip Schaff, *History of the Christian Church* (1910; repr. Grand Rapids: Eerdmans, 1979), 8:519; cited in Valentine Andreae, *Respublica Christianopolitana* (1642).

to interpreting faithfully a piece of music; rather, he is like a composer who borrows several themes and then orchestrates them according to his personal inspiration. Calvin makes the themes of Luther, Melanchthon, Zwingli, and Bucer resound at times *forte* and at other times *piano* and interprets them into a composition that is his own.[23]

Conclusion

Citizens on both sides of the Atlantic believed that the intellectual descendants of Calvin were the founders of colonial America. Friend and foe alike recognized the impact of Calvin and his Puritan followers. David Hume once admitted that, "for all the liberty of the English constitution that nation is indebted to the Puritans."[24] More positively describing the preaching of Pilgrim father John Norton, George Bancroft summarized:

> The political character of Calvinism, which, with one consent and with instinctive judgment, the monarchs of that day feared as republicanism, and which Charles II declared a religion unfit for a gentleman, is expressed by a single word—*predestination*. Did a proud aristocracy trace its lineage through generations of a high-born ancestry?—the republican reformer, with a loftier pride, invaded the invisible world, and from the book of life brought down the record of the noblest enfranchisement, decreed from all eternity by the King of kings.[25]

23. Alexandre Ganoczy, *The Young Calvin*, trans. David Foxgrover and Wade Provo (Philadelphia: Westminster Press, 1987), 232; cited by Will Barker in *A Theological Guide to Calvin's Institutes: Essays and Analysis* (Phillipsburg, NJ: P&R Publishing, 2008). Another Roman Catholic work that appreciates Calvin is Lucien Joseph Richard's *The Spirituality of John Calvin* (Atlanta, GA: John Knox Press, 1974).

24. Cited in A. W. M'Clure, *Lives of the Chief Fathers of New England* (Boston: Massachusetts Sabbath School Society, 1846), 2:134.

25. M'Clure, *Lives of the Chief Fathers of New England*, 219.

John Calvin, at his five hundredth birthday, is not the property of one denomination or religious tradition. His thought and work are far greater than that. The concerted testimony of many as outlined above illustrates how he transcends time and tradition. Perhaps in view of these tributes, the event-shaping life of Calvin, and his contributions which made a difference in culture, modern readers will better appreciate C. S. Lewis's call to comprehend "the freshness, the audacity, and the fashionableness of Calvinism."